The Journey of the Nomadic Soul
Rediscovering Tengrism

Allan Shepard

Booklas Publishing — 2025
"Work originally written in 2022."

Original Title:
The Journey of the Nomadic Soul – Rediscovering Tengrism
Copyright © 2025, published by Luiz Antonio dos Santos ME.
This book is a non-fiction work that explores practices and concepts within the field of ancestral spirituality and indigenous traditions of Central Asia. Through a profound and sensitive approach, the author reconstructs the foundations of Tengrism, a nomadic worldview centered on harmony between human beings, nature, and the sacred.

1st Edition

Production Team
Author: Allan Shepard
Editor: Luiz Santos
Cover Design: Studios Booklas / Lúcio Havel
Consultant: Ezra Dalmont
Researchers: Yuna Ferren / Ilias Corvan / Mateo Shurei
Layout Design: Nara Edrien
Translation: Helen Yorst

Publication & Identification
The Journey of the Nomadic Soul – Rediscovering Tengrism
Booklas, 2025
Categories: Spirituality / Ancestral Traditions
DDC: 299.511 — Asian-origin religions (Tengrism)
CDU: 299.51 — Specific religions: Turkic-Mongolic traditions

All rights reserved to:
Luiz Antonio dos Santos ME / Booklas
No part of this book may be reproduced, stored in a retrieval system, or transmitted in any form or by any means — electronic, mechanical, photocopying, recording, or otherwise — without the prior written permission of the copyright holder.

Summary

Systematic Index 5
Prologue 10
Chapter 1   Eternal Sky 14
Chapter 2   Ancient Roots 19
Chapter 3   Nomadic Soul 25
Chapter 4   God of the Sky 30
Chapter 5   Mother Earth 36
Chapter 6   Spirits of Nature 42
Chapter 7   Ancestral Veneration 48
Chapter 8   Three Worlds 54
Chapter 9   Celestial World 60
Chapter 10 Underworld 66
Chapter 11 Multiple Souls 72
Chapter 12 Shaman Mediator 78
Chapter 13 Sacred Rituals 84
Chapter 14 Shamanic Healing 90
Chapter 15 Totems and Symbols 96
Chapter 16 Sacred Sites 102
Chapter 17 Buddhist Syncretism 108
Chapter 18 Ancestral Resistance 114
Chapter 19 Tengri and Islam 120
Chapter 20 Tengri and Christianity 126
Chapter 21 Secular Modernity 132
Chapter 22 Current Revivalism 137

Chapter 23	Spiritual Search	143
Chapter 24	Siberian Shamanism	149
Chapter 25	Indigenous Traditions	155
Chapter 26	Ecological Vision	161
Chapter 27	Modern Practices	167
Chapter 28	Values and Ethics	174
Chapter 29	Spiritual Identity	180
Chapter 30	Sacred Connection	186
Chapter 31	Modern Re-signification	192
Chapter 32	Ancestral Wisdom	199
Chapter 33	Cosmic Harmony	206
Epilogue		212

Systematic Index

Chapter 1: Eternal Sky – Introduces Tengri, the Eternal Sky, as the supreme consciousness and core of Tengriist spirituality.

Chapter 2: Ancient Roots – Explores the historical origins and development of Tengriism among ancient nomadic cultures of the Eurasian steppes.

Chapter 3: Nomadic Soul – Details how Tengriism is intrinsically linked to the free, mobile, and nature-revering soul of nomadic peoples.

Chapter 4: God of the Sky – Focuses on the nature and role of Tengri, the supreme, formless Sky God who represents cosmic order and justice.

Chapter 5: Mother Earth – Introduces Mother Earth (Etugen) and Umay, emphasizing the vital role of the feminine divine and reverence for the land.

Chapter 6: Spirits of Nature – Details the belief in nature spirits (iye) inhabiting the landscape and the importance of respectful interaction with them.

Chapter 7: Ancestral Veneration – Explains the central practice of honoring ancestors (aruğ, ongod) and maintaining a living connection with the spirits of the dead.

Chapter 8: Three Worlds – Describes the Tengriist cosmology dividing existence into three interconnected realms: upper, middle, and lower worlds.

Chapter 9: Celestial World – Focuses on the upper realm, the dwelling place of Tengri, benevolent deities (like Ulgen, Mergen, Kayra), and elevated ancestral spirits.

Chapter 10: Underworld – Explores the concept of the underworld, its ruler Erlik Khan, and its role in transformation and cosmic balance.

Chapter 11: Multiple Souls – Discusses the complex belief in multiple souls composing a human being (nefes, shadow soul, sülde, etc.) and the concept of soul loss and retrieval.

Chapter 12: Shaman Mediator – Details the crucial role, calling, initiation, and practices of the shaman (kam, böö, udgan) as the mediator between worlds.

Chapter 13: Sacred Rituals – Describes key Tengriist rituals, including offerings, fire veneration, ovoo ceremonies, and life passage rites, emphasizing connection over dogma.

Chapter 14: Shamanic Healing – Focuses on shamanic healing methods, viewing illness as spiritual imbalance and involving soul retrieval and spirit negotiation.

Chapter 15: Totems and Symbols – Explores the significance of totemic animals (wolf, eagle, etc.) and core symbols like the World Tree, sun, moon, and colors in Tengriism.

Chapter 16: Sacred Sites – Discusses sacred natural sites like mountains and springs, the significance of ovoo, and the respectful interaction required.

Chapter 17: Buddhist Syncretism – Examines the historical syncretism between Tengriism and Tibetan Buddhism in Mongolia, resulting in "Yellow Shamanism."

Chapter 18: Ancestral Resistance – Details how Tengriism survived centuries of suppression through hidden practices, camouflage, and strategic syncretism ("Black Shamanism").

Chapter 19: Tengri and Islam – Discusses the interaction and syncretism between Tengriism and Islam among Turkic peoples, facilitated often by Sufism.

Chapter 20: Tengri and Christianity – Examines the historical encounter between Tengriism and Christianity, particularly Nestorianism, within the Mongol Empire.

Chapter 21: Secular Modernity – Addresses the suppression of Tengriism under 20th-century secular modernity, particularly Soviet communism, and its consequences.

Chapter 22: Current Revivalism – Details the contemporary resurgence and revival of Tengriism and shamanism in Central Asia and Siberia post-Soviet collapse.

Chapter 23: Spiritual Search – Explores the reasons behind the modern spiritual search and why Tengriism attracts contemporary seekers seeking connection and meaning.

Chapter 24: Siberian Shamanism – Focuses on the distinct yet related shamanic traditions of various Siberian peoples and their connection to Tengriism.

Chapter 25: Indigenous Traditions – Draws parallels between Tengriism and other indigenous spiritual traditions worldwide, highlighting shared core principles and worldviews.

Chapter 26: Ecological Vision – Highlights the inherent ecological ethic in Tengriism, viewing nature as sacred and emphasizing balance and reciprocity.

Chapter 27: Modern Practices – Details how Tengriism is practiced today, outlining adaptations like daily offerings, domestic shrines, and modern ritual forms.

Chapter 28: Values and Ethics – Outlines the core ethical values of Tengriism, emphasizing balance, honor, hospitality, and respect for nature and ancestors.

Chapter 29: Spiritual Identity – Explores the concept of spiritual identity within Tengriism, its suppression, rediscovery, and role in modern belonging and healing.

Chapter 30: Sacred Connection – Focuses on the core experience of sacred connection with the cosmos, nature, and spirits, lived through presence and simple rituals.

Chapter 31: Modern Re-signification – Discusses how Tengriist symbols, concepts, and practices are being reinterpreted and adapted for contemporary life and challenges.

Chapter 32: Ancestral Wisdom – Explores Tengriism as a form of living, embodied ancestral wisdom transmitted through practice, myth, and deep listening.

Prologue

We live in times where spirituality, for many, has become background noise. A diffuse memory. An almost imperceptible echo that, nonetheless, insists on calling — especially in the deepest moments of silence. Modernity, with its promises of progress, has distanced us from something essential. In the name of rationality, we have lost intimacy with the invisible. And so, thousands walk the world with an emptiness they cannot name. They miss something — they don't know what. But they feel it.

This absence, though subtle, reverberates in all spheres of life. Science, once skeptical about the subject, now confirms what the ancients knew intuitively: genuine spirituality not only nourishes the mind but also strengthens the body. Increasingly numerous clinical studies show that authentic spiritual practices — those that connect human beings with something greater than themselves — reduce stress levels, improve immunity, balance emotions, and enhance the sense of belonging. Spirituality, understood as an existential axis, is an invisible medicine.

And yet, many traditional religions have failed to keep this flame alive. They have become, for the most part, cumbersome, institutionalized, commercial systems. They speak of transcendence but offer rules. They promise reconnection but deliver cold liturgies. The temple has become a business. The sacred, a spectacle. And the human being, seeking spiritual shelter, finds empty corridors or automated voices.

It is in this scenario of searching and disconnection that a new silent trend imposes itself: the return to origins. Not as a regression to the past, but as a re-encounter with that which precedes modern systems. There is a growing movement of people seeking, in the remnants of ancient peoples, a living, fluid, organic spirituality. Among these forgotten — but never dead — traditions is Tengrism.

This book, which now rests in your hands, is an open door to this re-encounter.

Tengrism was not born in palaces nor revealed on sacred tablets. It emerged from the silence of the steppes, from the wind that sings between the mountains, from the instinctive reverence of the nomads before the sky. It is a spirituality that does not separate the sacred from the everyday. It *is* the everyday. It is in the way one touches the earth, how one thanks the animal that offers its life, how one listens to the council of the elders or the warning of dreams. It does not demand dogmas; it demands presence. And today, more than ever, this presence is urgent.

Reading this work, you will not merely be guided through historical accounts or anthropological descriptions. You will be touched by a wisdom that still pulsates, that has not been extinguished — only silenced. Each chapter is a reconnection with deep layers of the human experience. You will find here a spirituality that speaks directly to intuition, to the body, to the ancestral memory that still lives within us. Because yes — even amidst concrete walls and digital screens — we are still children of the sky and the earth.

Tengrism is, above all, a cosmovision: a way of perceiving the world as a living, interdependent organism. There is no hierarchy between human and nature — there is reciprocity. Rivers are beings, animals are guides, dreams are maps. The Sky is not a distant place onto which a punitive god is projected, but a comprehensive, living consciousness that observes in silence and speaks through cycles. The Earth, in turn, is Mother in the full sense — not a metaphor, but reality. Everything that is born, grows, dies, and is reborn, does so between these two pillars: Father Sky and Mother Earth.

This book is an invitation — but not one that expects your immediate response. It is a call that plants seeds. Perhaps you will read it entirely and only realize its effects months later. Perhaps something will touch you within the first few pages. In any case, your reading will not be innocuous. It awakens. It shifts. It heals.

As editor, it is not my place to dictate the value of a work. But I can affirm, with the experience of having read every line, that this text transcends the paper. It vibrates. It invokes. It reconnects us with what is essential and, at the same time, forgotten. Do not expect formulas, nor promises. What you will find here is truth — the kind of truth that doesn't shout, but whispers. And which, for that very reason, transforms.

Whatever your spiritual background, be certain: there is something here for you. A memory that needs to be reactivated. A fire that wishes to be fed. A wisdom that has always been yours, but which perhaps you have forgotten. Tengrism does not want to convert you. It merely offers a lens. And whoever sees through this lens perceives a world where everything — absolutely everything — is sacred.

Allow yourself to journey through these pages with an open soul. Not in haste, but with reverence. Listen to the silences. Feel the rhythm of the ancients. Recognize, in each paragraph, a mirror that reveals not the past, but the eternity that still pulsates now.

Luiz Santos, Editor

Chapter 1
Eternal Sky

The sky was not merely a vast blue expanse above the nomads' heads; it was the very consciousness of the universe. In every breath of wind across the steppes, in every ray of sun filtering through the clouds, one felt the presence of Tengri—the Eternal Sky, the supreme spirit that governed life and death with unperturbed silence.

On long journeys across the open fields of Central Asia, the eyes of the elders sought more than clouds or stars. They searched for signs, omens, answers. For in Tengriism, the sky is more than a cosmic backdrop: it is the living God itself, breathing upon the Earth.

The ancient Turkic and Mongol peoples did not build temples of stone. Their cathedrals were the mountains, their chapels the open valleys, and their altars the very ground beneath their feet. To live under Tengri was to live in harmony with the invisible order of things. The sky did not speak in words but manifested through natural cycles, climate changes, animal migrations, the course of rivers, and the arrangement of stars. For those who knew how to listen, the Sky was never silent.

Tengriist spirituality flourished amidst the winds of time without needing written doctrines or sacred scriptures. Its essence was oral, sensory, visceral. The sacred was not separate from the world; it spilled over onto everything. The shaman was not a priest of a book, but of experience. He read the signs of the sky, interpreted dreams, walked among the living and the dead, humans and spirits. He was a mediator between worlds, not because he held a title, but because his soul burned with the frequency of the unseen.

Tengri was not a being with a face or a name multiplied across languages. He was the deep blue of the firmament, the serene vibration hovering over all things. In Turkic and Mongolic languages, the word "Tengri" is simultaneously name and substance: it is the sky, it is the god, it is the principle of everything. It is the manifestation of order, justice, and life force. And though never depicted in human form, his presence was felt intensely in every birth, every harvest, every mourning.

Rituals performed on sacred mountains, atop *ovoos*—those piles of stones decorated with blue ribbons fluttering in the wind—were acts of communion with the Sky. There, the nomad offered *kumis*, the fermented horse milk, or burned juniper branches, invoking Tengri's protection. It wasn't about asking favors from a distant deity, but about aligning oneself with a cosmic force that already resided within one's own blood, breath, and destiny.

There was no sin in Tengriism. There was imbalance. There was a rupture with the natural cycle of things. Offending Tengri meant harming the world's harmony: disrespecting the earth, killing needlessly, acting dishonorably. Punishment wasn't imposed by a transcendental moral judgment but came in the form of failed harvests, diseases, storms—unequivocal signs that the connection with the Sky had been compromised.

In a world where so many religions compete for absolute truths, Tengriism offers another path: that of silent listening, humility before mystery, reverence for life in its broadest form. It demands no conversion, promises no salvation, separates no faithful from infidels. It invites belonging. To look at the sky and recognize oneself as part of it. To touch the earth and remember that from it we came and to it we shall return.

Today, as concrete replaces fields and artificial light hides the stars, many turn their eyes back to this ancient spiritual path. Amidst the noise of ideologies, the silent wisdom of the Eternal Sky is being heard once more. In the valleys of the Altai, on the plateaus of Mongolia, across the steppes of Kazakhstan, forgotten chants, dances, and rituals are reborn. Young people rediscover the names of the winds, the meanings of birds, the celestial maps etched into the souls of their ancestors.

For some, it is cultural resistance. For others, it is a response to the spiritual void of modernity. But for all, there is something deeply comforting in knowing that the sky has not abandoned us. That, even covered by satellites and electronic noise, we can still lift our eyes and find there the same blue vastness our ancestors revered. We can still, with humility and gratitude, say: "Tengri, Eternal Sky, I recognize you."

The return to Tengriism is not a return to the past, but a reconnection with the origin. It is not regression, it is regeneration. For the sky never ages. It never imposes itself. It simply is. Present. Watching. Guarding. Listening to prayers murmured on the wind.

And the wind still speaks. For those who know how to listen, it whispers ancient stories and eternal promises. It blows through the bones of the living and sings in the tombs of the dead. It carries the spirit of Tengri, invisible but ever-present, like a veil covering the Earth with dignity, justice, and hope.

Those who resume this path are not alone. Around the world, circles, rites, and gatherings under the open sky are growing. And every time someone, in any corner of the planet, lifts a stone, lights a fire, or pours milk upon the earth in reverence to the Sky, an ancient flame is rekindled. Not a flame of nostalgia, but of vigil. Of presence. Of a living link between the visible and the invisible. For the sky never fell. It is we who forgot to look up at it. And now, in remembering, in returning, we rediscover not just a religion, but a way of being in the world. A way of breathing, listening, being.

Restoring this ancient form of spirituality isn't just about rescuing customs or repeating ancestral ceremonies, but about finding an inner axis, a compass pointing beyond the daily noise. The return to Tengri is also a return to listening—listening to nature, the body, cycles, losses, and encounters. The contemporary shaman may no longer wear wolf skins or walk among smoky tents, but they carry within them the same ability to perceive the delicate stitching between worlds. The sacred resurfaces, thus, not as spectacle, but as a living presence in the simple gesture, in shared silence, in the awareness that everything is connected.

This reconnection doesn't require us to abandon our cities or technologies, but to change how we position ourselves before life. The sky, once the companion of nomads, can be the same sky contemplated from a high-rise window, as long as the eyes seeing it are open to its depth. The spirit of Tengri doesn't demand the steppe but asks for space within the soul. And perhaps this is the true modern challenge: to cultivate an interior vastness like the fields of Altai, to learn to see the divine in the invisible flows sustaining our existence, rescuing the reverence that precedes any word. Because in times of haste and forgetfulness, remembering the Eternal Sky is remembering oneself— not as a separate individual, but as part of a pulsating whole, ancient and ever new.

The path opening before those who recognize this truth is not written in stone nor drawn on maps. It is traced on the wind, revealed in the rhythm of the stars, sustained by the living memory of those who still dare to walk with eyes turned upward.

Chapter 2
Ancient Roots

Long before any word was written on parchment or any dogma carved in stone, the roots of Tengriism were already winding through the endless vastness of the Eurasian steppes. These roots did not spread by imposition or conquest but flourished naturally, like grass under the spring frost. They intertwined with the nomadic way of life, with the rhythms of the earth, with the winds crossing the prairies carrying secrets from forgotten ages. Tengriism was born where the sky touches the earth without intermediaries, among peoples who lived not under stone roofs, but beneath the blue dome of the eternal firmament.

Peoples like the Göktürks, the Xiongnu, the early Bulgars, and the Mongols found in Tengri not an abstract authority, but a direct reflection of the reality surrounding them. They were children of the sky and the steppe. To live was to move in circles—migrating with the seasons, following the herds, observing the stars. In this cosmic dance, every gesture was sacred. And Tengriism, more than a religion in the modern sense, was the invisible thread sewing together all aspects of existence. It was a worldview, an ethic, a memory.

The Orkhon inscriptions, carved into rocks in the 8th century, still echo like ancestral thunder on the banks of Mongolian rivers. They are not just historical records; they are spiritual testaments. There, one sees the clear conviction that the political power of the Turkic khagans came directly from Tengri. Leadership was not usurpation, but a celestial mandate. He who strayed from the path of the sky lost his right to rule, and misfortune was swift to fall upon his people. This conception reinforced a cosmic pact between the ruler and the sky—an invisible but indisputable contract.

Genghis Khan, the name that still resounds like thunder in the annals of time, never saw himself as a simple conqueror. He called himself the son of the Blue Sky. His rise, his victories, his mission in the world—all were understood as manifestations of Tengri's will. Atop the Burkhan Khaldun mountain, the young Temujin cried out to Tengri with tears and promises. There, between the stones and the heavens, an alliance was sealed that would guide the steps of the one who would become the unifier of tribes and the terror of empires.

But the Tengriism that inspired Genghis Khan was not a closed system, nor a fossilized doctrine. It was a fertile field, populated by a myriad of nature spirits, venerated ancestors, and chthonic entities. It was a fluid polytheism, where every river had a name, every mountain a guardian, every animal a spirit. Shamans, like gardeners of this invisible landscape, maintained the balance between worlds. With their drums and chants, they crossed the veils of ordinary reality to dialogue with the forces shaping the tribe's destiny.

This oral spirituality, transmitted by singers, storytellers, and elders, resisted time with the stubbornness of deep roots. Even without formal scriptures, it remained alive—because it was inscribed in daily practices, seasonal rites, social relations. Every birth was accompanied by protective rituals. Every marriage, by blessings from the sky. Every death, by chants guiding the soul to the domain of the ancestors. There was no separation between the sacred and the everyday.

And even as empires flourished and fell, even as organized religions advanced with missionaries and armies, Tengriism persisted. It adapted, hid, transformed, but never disappeared. During periods of Islamic and Buddhist influence, Tengriist elements were incorporated into the new systems. A sanctuary might become a mosque; an *ovoo*, a shrine. But the spirit whispering among the stones and in the grandmothers' songs remained the same.

Modern anthropological research reveals the complexity and depth of this ancestral religion. It cannot be reduced to mere animism or generic shamanism. It is, simultaneously, cosmic faith and spiritual ecology. A network of meanings connecting humans, animals, heavens, and lands in a living web. Its myths are not childish fables, but maps for understanding reality. Its rituals, far beyond symbolism, are tools for energetic rebalancing and communion with the whole.

During the times of Soviet domination, when traditional religions were persecuted and native culture suppressed, Tengriism survived in folk songs, proverbs, peasant customs. Milk was still poured onto the ground in silent offering. The wind was still greeted with reverence. Ancient names still echoed in secret baptisms. The steppe, silent and proud, guarded its spirituality like a fire kept under ashes.

Today, returning to these roots is not an archaeological return, but a reunion with something that never ceased to be present. Tengriism blossoms again not as exoticism or folkloric reconstruction, but as an authentic expression of a collective soul that has resisted the centuries. It emerges with the force of living memory, which needs not be reinvented, only remembered.

The ancient roots of Tengriism are, therefore, not only in the steppes or in the ruins of the Orkhon inscriptions. They are in the language spoken, in gestures repeated without knowing why, in the inexplicable longing for a time when the sky was everyone's roof and the wind was a counselor. They are in the eyes of those who, facing the vastness, understand that something greater is watching, guiding, waiting.

With every step taken on this sacred ground, with every breath under the deep blue sky, these roots renew themselves. They grow not downwards, but inwards. They sustain not trees, but consciousnesses. And in times when so many wonder who they are, where they come from, and where they are going, Tengriism offers an answer that comes not in ready-made phrases, but in silent presences: you are part of the whole. You came from the sky and the earth. And the way back is under your feet, written on the wind, tattooed on the clouds.

This subterranean force, which never needed walls or hierarchies to exist, resurfaces today not as a residue of a distant past, but as a beacon for a present searching for meaning. Unlike religions promising future worlds, Tengriism speaks of a sacred now—of an eternity pulsating in the instant, of a harmony that needs not be conquered, but recognized. It does not impose paths, only awakens a perception: that the human being is part of an ancestral current singing in every stone, every animal, every breath of air.

The return to this perception is not an abandonment of the modern world, but its reintegration with the invisible that sustains it. In communities where this knowledge remains alive, even if fragmented, one can perceive a sense of belonging that transcends time. It is not just ethnic pride or a search for identity; it is instinctive memory, as if souls carried in their silence the cadence of ancient drums. The young people who today listen to the teachings of the elders, who return to the valleys to light bonfires and celebrate the solstices, are not just reliving rituals—they are continuing a conversation begun millennia ago between the sky and the earth. They are responding to the call of something that never left them, just waited to be remembered.

And thus, in the slow rhythm of awakened memory, the roots assert themselves, not to bind, but to anchor. They do not limit, but offer direction. They are roots that nourish a way of being in the world where the sacred is found not on a distant altar, but in the gesture of one who respects the cycle of life. By resuming this ancestral path, one returns not only to the practices of the ancients, but to the deep listening of what still lives in them—and in us. For even beneath the skin of the present, the spirit of the steppes still walks, still sings, still dreams.

Chapter 3
Nomadic Soul

The soul of the nomadic peoples cannot be captured by simple words. It does not settle on definitions; it slips away like the wind through the cracks of a tent, walks alongside the cattle across the steppes, sleeps under the starry sky, and awakens with the first birdsong. This nomadic soul is, above all, free – and at the heart of this freedom pulses a spirituality without walls, dogmas, or borders: Tengriism.

Among the Mongols and Turks of Central Asia, religion was not a compartment isolated from life, like a temple visited at set times. It was a constant state of awareness. Everything was immersed in the sacred: the food gathered with effort, the fire that warmed, the horse that carried, the silence of the plain at dusk. Each element of daily life was an extension of the soul, and the soul was an inseparable part of the world. To live meant to coexist with greater forces, but never to submit blindly – it was a dialogue with nature, with spirits, with the sky itself.

Tribal organization reflected this view. There were no ecclesiastical hierarchies, no spiritual castes. The shaman was a mediator, not a dominator. The elder was a sage, not a legislator. Authority was born not from imposition, but from listening, experience, and mutual respect. The concept of hospitality, for example, transcended mere courtesy: receiving someone into one's home was recognizing that everyone belongs to the same spiritual family, all are children of Sky and Earth, all deserve shelter, food, and true words.

This religious experience was embodied in seasonal movements. Each season brought a new spiritual configuration. In summer, the green fields signaled Tengri's blessings; in winter, snow fell like a protective veil over living beings. Herding, an essential activity, was not just a means of subsistence, but also a rite. Choosing campsites involved observing animal behavior, cloud formations, visible stars. Time was circular – there was no beginning or end, only eternal renewal, in tune with the wheel of the sky.

The open sky above the plains instilled in the nomads an innate sense of reverence. It was impossible to look at the vastness and not feel something resonating within the chest – a call, a memory, a feeling of greater belonging. This sky was not a distant place, but a presence. Tengri, the Blue Sky, was the silent guardian, the incorruptible judge, the invisible father who watched without punishing, but also without being deceived. Every decision – a migration, a battle, a harvest – needed to be in tune with the sky's omens, the spirits' advice, the shamans' wisdom.

Not coincidentally, every mountain, every lake, every flock of birds carried spiritual significance. Rivers were veins of Mother Earth; winds, whispers of Father Sky. Killing an animal required a ritual of permission;

cutting down a tree, a prayer of thanks. The world was not a resource, but a relative. And respect was not imposed – it was intuitive. Those living on the steppe knew that arrogance was punished not by wrathful gods, but by nature itself: an untimely blizzard, a prolonged drought, a sickened herd. Balance was the only law, and imbalance, the only transgression.

This way of living and believing created a silent but profoundly effective moral code. The brave were respected, but the arrogant were avoided. The generous were honored, but the greedy were forgotten. The careful steward of the land was admired; the destroyer, cursed. This nomadic ethos was taught not with books, but with examples. Children learned by observing: how the father rode the horse, how the mother tended the fire, how the elders conversed with the wind.

Inside the felt tents, called *yurts* or *gers*, the central fire represented more than warmth: it was the heart of the home, the connection to ancestors, the linking point between worlds. Lighting the fire was a ritual act. Speaking loudly near it was considered disrespectful. Pouring water on the flames, a grave offense. The fire was masculine and feminine, earthly and celestial, purifying and communicative. Around it, families gathered to share stories, healings, songs – and thus, spirituality was transmitted, like an ember passing from one piece of wood to another without extinguishing.

This fusion of life and belief is perhaps the most striking feature of Tengriism. It was not a religion demanding blind faith, but an experience requiring presence. The sky was there, every day, changing color, announcing shifts, responding without words. The nomadic soul knew how to listen. And because it knew how to listen, it knew how to live.

When shamans entered trances, dancing to the drum's sound, they did not isolate themselves in temples; they did so before the clan, under the open sky, with the wind as witness. The community followed, not as spectators, but as participants. Each drumbeat was like the earth's pulse, each chant, a thread cast between worlds. The omens received there guided decisions that could change everyone's destiny.

The constant mobility of nomads did not distance them from spirituality – on the contrary, it allowed faith to remain alive and vibrant. There was no forgetting the sacred when one walked upon it, slept enveloped by it, depended on it for each new day. The path was temple. The horizon was altar. And the journey itself was prayer.

Today, in cities built over ancient caravan routes, many feel an undefined longing. It is the echo of the nomadic soul, still vibrating beneath the asphalt, still whispering among poles and antennas. This soul has not died. It merely fell silent. But a few days outdoors, a few moments of silence before the sky, and it awakens. Remembers. Recognizes. And finds again, in the innermost part of being, the trail back to the great blue field where everything began.

This reunion does not demand the literal reconstruction of a lifestyle, but invites an inner return, an attentive listening to what modernity tried to silence:

instinct, communion, humility before the unknown. Amidst the hustle of busy days, the nomadic soul can still live – not necessarily traversing infinite steppes, but rescuing the fluidity, lightness, and attention that guided the ancients. It's about moving with meaning, not fixing on rigid certainties, accepting the cycle as master and the sky as mirror. It's possible to be nomadic without leaving one's place, when carrying within oneself respect for the forces sustaining the world.

The wisdom of these peoples remains not as a museum piece, but as an ever-present invitation to live with wholeness. The fire may be symbolic, but its warmth is real: it lies in listening between generations, in sincere sharing, in caring for what nourishes and warms. Within each person lies the possibility of rekindling this invisible center, of rebuilding the home where spirituality and daily life touch. What the nomads taught with their steps is that faith is carried not in books, but in gestures. That sacredness needs no ornaments, only presence. And perhaps this is the greatest legacy of the nomadic soul: the certainty that the path matters more than the destination. That life need not be dominated, only understood in its eternal dance of change and permanence. The sky remains where it always was, and the wind, even today, sings ancient names in attentive ears. It is up to us to decide whether we want merely to survive within walls, or live fully under the same firmament that guided the steps of those who came before.

Chapter 4
God of the Sky

Tengri. No other name spoken among the nomadic peoples of Central Asia evoked such reverent silence. And not because there was fear, but because there was recognition. Tengri was not a distant god to be feared; nor was he a humanized entity demanding servitude. He was the Sky itself – blue, vast, infinite, serene. A power that asserted itself not through force, but through presence.

Unlike deities carved in temples, Tengri was never represented by human hands. He did not fit into forms, reside in images, or allow himself to be reduced to symbols. His dwelling was the firmament itself. His altar, the celestial vault. His language, cosmic silence.

The word "Tengri," in Turco-Mongol languages, carries a duality: it denotes both the physical sky and the supreme consciousness inhabiting it. There is no separation between matter and spirit. The blue sky stretching over the steppes is not just an atmospheric layer – it is spirit, consciousness, divinity. Calling him "Father Sky" is not metaphor; it is spiritual realization. And onto this Father, human traumas or expectations are not projected. He does not punish with wrath, nor reward with favoritism. He observes, maintains order, sustains the eternal cycle of life and death.

Kök Tengri – the "Blue Sky" – was seen as the highest of powers. But even this word "power" must be handled with care. Tengri did not dominate; he permeated. His supremacy was not based on coercion, but on harmony. The cosmic order, called *törü* among the ancient Turks, was the expression of the balance desired by Tengri. To break this order – to lie, act greedily, disrespect nature – was to go against the Sky. And there was no need for intermediaries to know this: one only had to look within, and look up.

In ancient imperial traditions, the khagans received their authority directly from Tengri. The ideal ruler was not the strongest, nor the most astute – but the one who best reflected the Sky's will. This deeply rooted concept made political power an extension of spiritual order. The khagan was not just a military chief; he was the link between the people and the Sky. His actions needed to align with cosmic justice. If there was drought, plague, or defeat in war, it was understood that the ruler had lost Tengri's favor. It was, therefore, time for change.

This celestial legitimacy was confirmed by rituals, visions, and oracles. The shaman, in trance, could hear the Sky's call and identify the chosen one. Often, a leader emerged from the least expected – not by heredity, but by spiritual merit. Genghis Khan, for example, claimed to have received his destiny directly from Tengri. His victory was not just human conquest, but the expression of a higher design. And this belief was not mere propaganda – it was lived as reality. When warriors rode under the blue sky, they did not do so only with weapons; they carried the invisible blessing of the Eternal Sky.

Beneath Tengri existed other deities and spirits. But none rivaled his supremacy. They were lesser manifestations – sometimes forces of nature, sometimes deified ancestors, sometimes tutelary entities. But always subordinate to the Blue Sky. The spiritual structure of Tengriism, though flexible, recognized a clear hierarchy: Tengri above all, then the celestial powers, the earth spirits, and finally, human beings. But even humans, with all their fragility, could access the Sky's wisdom – simply by being in harmony with it.

This accessibility made Tengri both transcendent and intimate. He needed no churches, dogmas, or priests. One only had to raise one's eyes. Listen to the wind. Feel justice in one's own actions. It was possible to speak with Tengri from a mountaintop or before a domestic hearth. It was possible to ask for protection when crossing a storm or give thanks for a successful birth. Tengri was always present, but never invasive.

The language used to refer to him reveals much about this relationship. "Möngke Tengri," the Eternal Sky, was called upon to witness solemn oaths. When someone lied in his name, it was said that the sky itself would turn against that person – and winds, drought, illness would come as impersonal retaliation. Not out of vengeance, but as a restoration of order. It was the expression of natural justice, not the wrath of a wounded god.

Rituals dedicated to Tengri involved no dogmas or fixed liturgies. They were acts of connection. Sacrificing a white horse – a symbol of purity and nobility – was one of the deepest forms of reverence. This sacrifice, however, was not performed lightly. It required ceremony, fasting, purity of intention. And even then, it was not the blood itself that pleased the Sky, but the sincerity of the gesture. In modern times, these rituals have been replaced by symbolic offerings – milk, *kumis*, tobacco, blue stones. The essence remains: recognizing the gift of life, returning part to the universe, maintaining the flow.

The absence of a physical form attributed to Tengri was never a sign of limitation, but of transcendence. He was all forms and none. He was the movement of planets, the silence of night, the horizon line. Comparing him to the Chinese concept of Tian is valid to a point – both represent the Sky as an ordering principle – but Tengri carries a unique quality: he is both destiny and path. Not an entity judging after death, but a presence guiding at every moment of life.

Spirituality centered on Tengri creates no separations between heaven and earth, sacred and profane. It teaches that everything is a manifestation of the same principle. That every gesture counts. That every word spoken under the sky is heard. That every action carries cosmic consequences. Thus, living in accordance with Tengri is more than a belief – it is an ethic. A way of being in the world with respect, dignity, and awareness.

In present days, when the divine is often sought in elaborate words or complicated institutions, Tengri's call sounds with cutting simplicity. Look at the sky. Breathe deeply. Act truthfully. Give thanks. Protect. The wisdom of the Eternal Sky need not be deciphered – it needs to be lived.

This experience, anchored in simplicity and wholeness, invites not passive contemplation, but deep engagement with life as it is. Tengri demands not renunciation, but presence. Not blind faith, but coherence between thought, feeling, and action. In a world saturated with images, discourses, and promises, his strength lies precisely in not being visible—but perceptible. He does not appear, but reveals himself. And he reveals himself in minimal gestures: in the way we treat animals, step on the earth, look into others' eyes. Every moment can be an altar, if inhabited with awareness.

The return to this spirituality of the Sky does not mean refusing the achievements of the present, but re-enchanting one's gaze. It is possible to live among machines and memories, technology and tradition, and still maintain the listening to the invisible. Tengri did not disappear with the advance of cities—he merely fell silent amidst the noise. But a moment of true silence is enough for him to be felt again. And when this happens, it is not a thunderous revelation, but an internal settling. As if something within the chest, long misaligned, finally finds its axis. Its direction. For the Sky remains where it always was—vast, blue, infinite. And its message remains clear, even if many have forgotten how to hear it.

Living under Tengri is remembering that every life is part of a larger order. It is assuming the sacred responsibility for every choice, every word, every silence. And in doing so, one is not just revering an ancestral god, but re-approaching an essential truth: that we are all children of the Sky and the Earth—and that walking between them, with dignity, is all the Sky expects of us.

Chapter 5
Mother Earth

If the sky is the eternal father observing silently from above, the earth is the living mother welcoming with fertile arms every step, every seed, every sigh. At the heart of Tengriist spirituality, this duality is not opposition – it is union. The human being is not born of chance or impersonal processes: he sprouts from the sacred union between the Blue Sky and the Dark Earth. A cosmic marriage that not only gives rise to life but sustains the balance of all that exists.

Etugen, Mother Earth, is the goddess whose presence pulses in every hill, every forest, every grave where the dead rest and grains germinate. She is not seen as a distant or abstract figure. She is alive, tangible, present. Her womb is the soil, her breath the gentle winds, her blood the rivers. For the nomadic peoples of Central Asia, honoring Etugen was as essential as revering Tengri. If the sky was invoked with eyes raised, the earth was revered with bare feet and hands dipped in mud.

Turco-Mongol tradition preserves another female figure of immense power: Umay, the protector of childhood and fertility. While Etugen represents the cosmic womb, Umay watches over newborns and presides over births. She is invoked by mothers, celebrated in soft chants, recognized in the warmth of the hearth and the security of a mother's embrace. Her name echoes in amulets, embroideries, and blessings passed down through generations. Among shamans, she is seen as a guiding spirit protecting children until they grow and can connect with Sky and Earth on their own.

These female figures are not secondary appendages of a male-dominated pantheon. They are central, vital, indispensable. In Tengriism, the complementarity between masculine and feminine is not a theoretical construct – it is a living reality. Sky and Earth do not compete, they coexist. Father Sky provides the spirit, Mother Earth gives the body. Life is born from the joining of the two. And therefore, respect for the earth is not just a matter of ecology – it is filial reverence, a recognition that we tread upon the very flesh of the goddess who bore us.

In times of sowing, nomads sang hymns of gratitude to the Earth. When a pasture yielded beyond expectation, it was considered that Etugen was pleased. But if there was drought, if the land dried up, it was understood that something had been broken: perhaps a local spirit was offended, perhaps an offering had been forgotten. Correcting this was more than a rite – it was a moral duty. Fresh milk was poured upon the earth. Golden grains were buried as an offering. Juniper incense was lit in the fields. Each gesture carried intention: to ask forgiveness, renew the bond, restore harmony.

For the nomad, the earth was not property. It was kin. More than that: it was mother. And with a mother, one does not negotiate, exploit, or dominate. With a mother, one coexists. Shares. Cares. This view permeates the entire nomadic way of life: cities are not built, for laying foundations is like driving stakes into the mother's body. One moves from season to season, allowing fields to breathe, nature to recover. This mobility is not just pragmatic – it is spiritual. It is the way not to overburden the mother with human demands.

Mountains, particularly, were seen as the breasts of Mother Earth. From them flowed pure waters, life, refuge. Clans often chose a tutelary mountain – not just as a point of orientation, but as a living entity that protected and inspired. Climbing the mountain at certain times of the year was a pilgrimage. Upon reaching the summit, devotees left offerings, sang, conversed with local spirits. This was not superstition, but an experience of direct connection. One felt the pulse of the Earth. One heard her voice, even in silence.

In wedding rituals, shamans often called upon Sky and Earth as witnesses. The union of two people mirrored the cosmic union that originated the world. The home built from this marriage was seen as a microcosm of the universal order. The fire lit in the tent was the heart of the Earth fed by the breath of the Sky. And therefore, any act of disrespect within the home – violence, lies, selfishness – was interpreted as a breach of cosmic harmony. Punishment came not through external chastisements, but through internal disorder: infertility, illness, misfortune.

The sacred perception of the earth also imposed clear limits on human action. Hunt only what is necessary. Never kill pregnant females. Gather plants carefully, thanking the plant's spirit. Do not pollute rivers, nor spill blood in sacred places. Every action had weight. Every gesture could strengthen or weaken the relationship with the Mother. Therefore, among the most ancient peoples, there were stories teaching these values through myths: the hunter who killed excessively and was devoured by wolves, the man who offended the mountain and lost his children, the woman who did not honor Umay and had her dreams stolen.

In the contemporary world, these narratives may seem symbolic, but for nomads, they were lived literally. The Earth was alive. It had moods, cycles, justice. When happy, it offered everything. When offended, it withdrew its sustenance. And this was not punishment – it was simply response.

This view produced highly sustainable societies. They lived with little, but with inner abundance. They knew what to harvest, what to leave. They respected the signs, did not force the times. Was there hunger? One learned to wait. Was there cold? One thanked the mother for shelter. Every natural challenge was a lesson, not a war. Because warring against the earth is warring against oneself. And Tengriism always knew this.

In the present, this ancestral wisdom begins to reawaken. When the soil cries for help, when water becomes scarce, when cities suffocate in concrete, the heirs of Mother Earth remember that there is an ancient, tested, effective path: the path of reverence. Not exploitation. Not consumption. But loving care, deep respect, silent gratitude. Rescuing Etugen is not returning to the past, but recovering the lost link between humanity and nature. It is recognizing that we own nothing, are merely passengers in the generous womb of a goddess who, even wounded, still waits for reconciliation.

Mother Earth still breathes beneath our feet. Still sings through the winds. Still weeps for the burned forests. But she also smiles when we treat her kindly.

In times of ecological urgency and growing alienation, the spirituality embodied in the figure of Etugen offers more than a religious alternative: it offers a paradigm. A way of seeing and living that repositions the human in its true dimension—not as the center of the world, but as part of a living, ancestral, sacred network. This paradigm is not imposed by dogmas, but blossoms from the recognition that life, in all its forms, is an expression of the same mother. Reverence for the Earth is not an abstract ideal: it is a daily practice, a way of acting that begins with small gestures and extends to major choices.

Turning our eyes back to Mother Earth is, therefore, relearning to listen. Listening to the body's signals, the rhythms of the seasons, the silence of the mountains. It is perceiving that walking on the ground is not a trivial act, but a reunion with an ancient womb still pulsating beneath our feet. It is possible to live in cities and still honor Etugen—simply by cultivating respect, listening, and care. It is not about nostalgia, but reconnection. For what was lived wisely by the nomadic peoples belongs not only to the past: it belongs to any time when humans wish to live in harmony with what sustains them.

Mother Earth demands not praise, but awareness. Her plea is simple, her language clear: care to continue. Listen to remain. Thank to belong. When we understand this, spirituality ceases to be a search for answers and becomes a practice of presence. Etugen teaches us that the ground we walk on is also the ground we will become, and that respect for the Earth is, ultimately, respect for our own origin. Because living with her, not against her, is the first step on any path that truly aims for wisdom.

Chapter 6
Spirits of Nature

The landscape stretching endlessly under the blue sky is not silent. Though to modern ears it may seem empty, it is filled with voices. Voices that speak not in human languages, but in breezes, movements, presences. At the heart of Tengriism, this understanding is alive: the natural world is not just scenery. It is inhabited, conscious, full of intentions. Every stone, every river, every tree holds a spirit. These nature spirits, called *iye*, are not symbolic concepts or folkloric beings – they are real, sensitive entities with their own will, with whom humans must coexist respectfully.

For the Turkic and Mongol peoples, nature was a great living body. Each element – water, fire, earth, air – was animated by an invisible force. The *iye* were the guardians of these elements. A lake was not just a mirror of water: it was the dwelling place of a consciousness. A mountain was not just a geographical elevation: it was the throne of an ancestral spirit. And just as one owes respect to an elder or a guest, one also owes respect to these invisible beings. Because, although unseen, they watch. And respond.

Each nomadic tribe knew the *iye* of its region. There were rivers that could not be crossed without prayer. Trees that could not be cut without offering. Rocks that could not be moved without permission. Sometimes, a spring was called "grandmother of the clan." Sometimes, a solitary stone in the middle of the steppe was considered a spiritual sentinel. These places became meeting points between the visible and the invisible. They were altars without walls, temples without doors.

Shamans knew the names of these spirits. They knew how to invoke them, calm them, offer them what they liked: milk, fat, tobacco, songs, silence. When a clan arrived at a new pasture, it was the shaman's duty to introduce himself to the local *iye*, declare peaceful intentions, ask for permission. And when something went wrong – a sudden illness, a strange accident, an unsettling premonition – it was said that a local spirit had been offended. The remedy was not just physical: the bond needed to be restored.

These rites did not follow universal formulas. They were intimate, local, transmitted orally through lineage. Some spirits demanded absolute silence. Others liked music. Some revealed themselves in dreams. Others in animal behaviors. A wolf howling differently. A bird flying against the wind. A dog refusing to enter a certain area. All this was read as a message. Because the *iye* speak not with voices, but with signs.

Among living creatures, certain animals were considered special manifestations of these spirits. The wolf, for example, was seen as an ancestral guide. The horse, as a messenger between worlds. The eagle, as the eye of Tengri. There were entire clans that adopted an animal as a spiritual totem – not out of idolatry, but spiritual affinity. It was believed that the spirits of totemic animals protected their human descendants, guided them in battles, appeared in dreams to warn or advise. And this was not allegory: it was lived as reality.

Killing an animal, therefore, was not a trivial action. A ritual of gratitude was necessary. Apologize to the animal's spirit, promise that nothing would be wasted, sing a song of honor. It was common for the hunter to place a handful of grass in the mouth of the dead animal – as food for its soul on its spiritual journey. The bones were treated with respect, often returned to the earth or kept in sacred places. Because the dead animal was not a "thing"; it was a being. And the spirit was still watchful.

Likewise, ancient trees were treated as silent sages. Felling a tree without reason was a serious transgression. Planting a tree, a meritorious act. Among Mongols and Buryats, certain forests were called "soul groves" – places where the presences were so dense that merely entering required reverence. No one shouted. No one hunted. One simply walked in silence, feeling observed, and perhaps, blessed.

Storms, earthquakes, frosts – none of this was attributed to chance. They were manifestations of angered or agitated *iye*. When lightning cut the sky in threatening zigzags, it was said that spirits were in dispute. When the wind blew contrary to the season, it was because something needed correction in human behavior. The shaman was called. Offerings were made.

The clan gathered in prayer. And order, almost always, was restored.

The relationship with nature spirits also shaped morality. Polluting a river was not only an environmental offense but a spiritual one. Shouting near a spring was seen as disrespectful. Urinating or spitting in sacred places, a profanation. Even the act of defecating required choosing a distant spot, respecting the spirit of the earth. And in larger ceremonies, offered foods were prepared with extreme care, as they nourished not only the living but the invisible.

In ancient narratives, there are stories of *iye* who saved entire tribes – warning of dangers, offering shelter in caves, teaching safe paths during migrations. There are also accounts of *iye* who punished the arrogant without mercy – drying up springs, killing cattle, driving them mad. But in all cases, the common thread is clear: respect brings blessings, disrespect brings misfortune. The spirits are neither good nor bad – they are just. And attentive.

Today, amidst concrete and noise, many have lost this sensitivity. Nature has been reduced to a resource, animals to products, forests to statistics. But in certain hearts, memory resurfaces. Someone feels a shiver upon entering a wood. Someone dreams repeatedly of the same animal. Someone, without knowing why, decides to plant a tree and sing to it. In these small reconnections, the call of the *iye* still lives.

Tengriism, with its ancestral wisdom, offers a path of reunion. It demands not blind belief, but openness of perception. It invites listening to the earth, observing the sky, dialoguing with the wind. It teaches that we are not alone, nor does the world serve us. We are intertwined in an invisible network, where each spirit has its place, function, voice.

Coexistence with nature spirits, as proposed by Tengriism, occurs not only on the plane of worship or caution. It shapes an ethic that transcends conventional morality, as it presupposes active listening to the surrounding world, full attention to the subtle signs permeating daily life. The gesture of offering milk to the earth or the respectful silence before a centuries-old tree are not obsolete or folkloric practices: they are expressions of a sensitivity that recognizes the sacred in all that exists.

In this worldview, spirituality is not a domain separate from life, but its very fabric, intertwining the human and non-human in bonds of reciprocity. This way of seeing transforms the very idea of existence. It's not just about living *in* the world, but living *with* the world. The boundaries between the visible and invisible become porous, and reality gains symbolic density. An animal crossing the path, a stone catching the eye, a sudden gust of wind – everything can carry a message, everything can be a vehicle of presence. Life, then, is a constant dialogue with spirits, and attention becomes a form of prayer.

It is in this fertile field of listening and reverence that a spirituality blossoms which does not separate, but unites; which does not impose, but invites. Thus, the call of the *iye* still echoes, even in times of steel and glass. They persist in dreams that trouble us, in landscapes that move us for no apparent reason, in small gestures carrying ancient intuition. Reconnecting with these spirits requires not a return to the past, but a return to the sensible – relearning to be in the world with humility and presence. Because for those who listen with an open heart, nature has never stopped speaking.

Chapter 7
Ancestral Veneration

Among the nomads of the steppe, death was never absence. It did not end a cycle; it transformed it. The breath leaving the body did not dissolve into nothingness but remained alive, sensitive, attentive. The dead did not go to a distant beyond, but to a parallel dwelling – invisible, yet accessible. And the living, in their millennial wisdom, knew that ignoring the dead would break the line sustaining the continuity of the world. At the heart of Tengriism, honoring ancestors was not an act of nostalgia. It was a pact of loyalty. It was keeping the link intact between what was, what is, and what is yet to come.

Aruğ was the name given to the spirits of great leaders, warriors, and shamans who, after death, did not fade but ascended to a position of spiritual protection over their clan. These lord-spirits became silent counselors, invisible guardians. Before battles, migrations, or important decisions, nomads invoked them, seeking signs and blessings. They were like deep roots sustaining the community's tree – unseen, but essential.

Below the *aruğ* were the closer spiritual protectors, often former shamans or wise women of the clan who had mastered the arts of the spirit in life and thus continued to intercede after death. Among the Mongols, they were called *ongod*. These beings were called during specific rituals, and often manifested through the bodies of living shamans, lending them strength, voice, and vision. The shaman did not merely represent the ancestor – he was temporarily possessed by him. This temporary fusion was viewed not with fear, but with reverence. The community gathered around the drum, the fire, the juniper smoke, and there, in the shaman's dance, recognized the movement of ancestry.

And further down, but no less important, were the common ancestors: parents, grandparents, great-grandparents – those whose memory was alive within the family, even if their actions hadn't echoed in epic deeds. These ancestors formed an intimate network of protection. Their spirits linked to specific places: a hill where they used to camp, a river where they fished, a tree where they rested. These locations became sacred. And whenever a family passed by, they left offerings, lit a flame, spoke words of gratitude. Not to maintain a custom, but to maintain a conversation.

Because ancestral veneration in Tengriism is exactly that: a dialogue. The dead listen, respond, teach. There is no rigid separation between the living and the dead – there is transit. A birth could be interpreted as the return of a family soul. A vivid dream could contain a warning from a great-grandfather. A child who, without ever learning them, spoke ancient words was considered touched by the memory of those who came before.

Ancestry was not static – it was active, entangled in the present.

In every home, there were small domestic altars. They were not elaborate – a special stone, a bowl of milk, a fragment of bone. At night, especially during seasonal periods, the family gathered to feed the fire and whisper names. This naming was a powerful rite. It was said that the spirit lives only as long as it is remembered by name. Therefore, ancestral names were passed on: a son might be named after his grandfather. Not by chance, but for renewal. Because the name carries energy, destiny, presence.

The fire was the main link. The hearth lit in the center of the tent was more than heating: it was the spiritual axis of the lineage. It was never allowed to go out without reason. One never spat or pointed at it. When lighting it, a prayer was made. When feeding it with fat or dried dung, thanks were given. It was before the flame that the dead were called. And it was not uncommon for the shaman, in an altered state, to say: "He is here," referring to a beloved ancestor. In that moment, time stopped. The past descended. The present opened. Eternity manifested in the warmth of the flame.

Even the great conquerors – like Genghis Khan – were incorporated into this spiritual network. After his death, the Khan of Khans did not become just a historical figure. He became an *ongod*. Protector of the Mongol people, tutelary spirit of entire clans. Rituals were performed in his memory not as official ceremony, but as an act of spiritual devotion. It is said that on certain new moon nights, one can still hear the drums on

Burkhan Khaldun – as if Temujin's steps still echoed, seeking to remind the living of their celestial origin.

The transmission of this devotion was oral, but carried weight. A father told his son how his grandfather had hunted the sacred bear. A grandmother taught her granddaughter the right words to greet the spirit of her great-grandfather when lighting incense. Each generation was a repository of living memory. Not memorizing was breaking. Forgetting was betrayal. Therefore, the elders were listened to patiently. Because from them came the bridge.

This veneration also imposed conduct. It was not enough to pray. One had to live in a way that honored the ancestors. A shameful act stained the entire lineage. A noble gesture uplifted everyone. The dead were silent judges – not vengeful, but demanding. They expected righteousness, courage, generosity. They expected the living to care for the land, the animals, the tribal pacts. Not to lie in vain. Not to dishonor the inherited name.

During seasonal festivals, like the summer solstice, there were public offerings to the ancestors. Entire groups gathered, wearing ceremonial attire, bringing food, milk, vodka. They danced, sang, wept. But above all, they listened. The shaman's drum was the beat of the collective heart. The rising smoke was the thread of return. And there, even among the youngest, a deep sense of belonging blossomed.

Today, in modern cities, ancestral veneration has not disappeared – it has merely hidden. It might be in the grandmother's photo on the shelf. In food prepared exactly as the great-grandfather liked. In the recurring dream of a deceased aunt. In the premonition that something needs to be done "in honor" of someone who has departed. These are seeds of the ancient practice – still latent, still fertile.

The contemporary revival of Tengriism has strongly rescued this dimension. In Siberian villages, Mongolian communities, Kazakh plains, families are relighting ceremonial hearths. Returning to ancient tombs. Rebuilding altars. Recording genealogies. Because they know that without roots, there is no tree. And without ancestry, there is no identity.

Honoring ancestors is recognizing that the self is just one link. That each of our gestures carries the weight and hope of those who came before. That our victories are collective achievements. And our failures, wounds that reverberate. But above all, it is knowing that we are never alone. With every step, thousands of spirits walk with us. Silent, yes. Invisible, perhaps. But alive – as alive as the wind that moves the tents and souls of the steppe.

Understanding ancestral veneration through the lens of Tengriism makes it clear that it is not limited to a belief system: it is a way of living time, a spiritual architecture of belonging. The continuity between the living and the dead is not a poetic metaphor, but a structural pillar of existence. The past does not rest behind—it pulses within, manifests in decisions, affections, gestures. Ancestry, in this context, demands not only ceremonial reverence, but ethical presence: active listening to memory and real responsibility for what we inherit from it.

The strength of this bond reveals itself mainly at life's crossroads. When there is doubt, fear, or change, the link with ancestors becomes a compass. Not out of superstition, but because therein lies accumulated knowledge, wisdom transcending the individual and anchored in collective experience. Invoking a hunter grandfather before a crossing, repeating a grandmother's song in difficult times, recognizing an ancestor's mistakes as lessons not to repeat – all this is a living update of the lineage. And in this gesture of return and listening, the notion of identity forms not as something invented, but remembered.

This remembrance is, ultimately, a form of love. Loving those who came before is accepting that we are part of a current that did not begin with us and will not end with us. It is carrying names with dignity, lighting flames with care, walking upright because ancient eyes are watching us, not to judge, but to sustain. Thus, ancestral veneration is not ritualized longing – it is deep trust: that we do not walk alone, but in the company of an invisible multitude that, with every gust of wind and every crackle of ember, whispers that we are on the right path.

Chapter 8
Three Worlds

The nomadic soul did not walk only upon the visible steppes. Its steps echoed across multiple layers of reality. At the heart of Tengriism, existence is conceived as a great living tree, whose roots delve into the underworld, trunk sustains earthly life, and branches open to the infinite sky. This structure is not allegory: it is spiritual perception. The ancient nomads of Central Asia did not see reality as flat, singular, but as a tripartite cosmos, where each world has its inhabitants, laws, and sacredness. These three worlds – upper, middle, and lower – are separated not by distance, but by vibration, level of consciousness, function in the balance of the whole.

The middle world, where humans live, is just the visible band of this great cosmic tree. Above stretches the celestial world, domain of Tengri and the elevated forces. Below rests the lower world, where dark spirits, wandering souls, and energies of transformation dwell. The human being, born into the middle world, stands exactly between these two forces: a vertical tension impelling him towards both elevation and fall, light and shadow, sky and earth.

In the spiritual imagination of the Turkic and Mongol peoples, this cosmology took concrete form. A World Tree was imagined rising at the center of the universe. This tree was not an abstract symbol, but a living presence. Its roots pierced the bowels of the underworld, its sap flowed through visible reality, and its crown reached the stars. It was called by various names: *Ulmo, Bodga Mod, Eje*, depending on the ethnic group. But its role was always the same: axis of the world, connection between realms, path of the shamans.

Shamans, uniquely capable of consciously traversing between worlds, knew the invisible geography of these realms. During their rituals, to the sound of the drum and invocations, they symbolically climbed the tree's branches or descended its roots. Each level of the celestial world was inhabited by spirits of light, virtuous ancestors, sky gods. These levels were not homogeneous: seven heavens, or even nine, were often spoken of, each with its functions and entities. At the apex of the highest heaven resided Kayra, the original creator, or even Tengri himself in his purest, impersonal form.

The underworld, conversely, was described as an inverted mirror of the earth. It possessed dark rivers, cold forests, lightless caves. There dwelt restless spirits, chaotic beings, commanded by Erlik Khan, the lord of the depths. Fear of the underworld was not fear of moral damnation, as in Western theologies, but apprehension of disorder, dissolution, oblivion. The soul falling into the underworld was not necessarily evil, but unbalanced, confused, burdened with unresolved weight.

The middle world, where humans live, was understood as a space of mediation. Here, the three worlds meet. And therefore, every human gesture has cosmic repercussion. How one treats the earth, fire, animals, the pledged word—all affects not only present life, but also the upper and lower worlds. An act of kindness resonates in the celestial spheres; a spiritual offense can open cracks for dark forces to escape the underworld.

This vertical view of reality did not produce fear, but responsibility. The nomad who knew the cosmology of the three worlds knew he lived in a network of reciprocity. He was not the center of the universe, but a link. And his duty was to maintain balance.

The shaman's drum – with its round surface and marked rim – often bore drawings of the three worlds: stars above, animals and rivers in the middle, serpents at the roots. When the drum sounded, it was as if the World Tree vibrated. And the worlds opened.

Nomadic homes, the yurts, also symbolized this structure. The skylight at the top – the *töönö* – represented the opening to the sky. The central fire was the heart of the middle world. The ground beneath the feet, the connection to the lower world. Living in a yurt was thus living within a microcosm, in harmony with the triple structure of the universe. Therefore, rituals performed in the tent assumed special force: each chant, each smoke, each offering reached the three planes simultaneously.

Childhood, maturity, and old age were also viewed through this cosmological lens. The child came from the celestial world – a newly arrived soul, still carrying brightness. The adult mediated the worlds – facing the challenges of the middle. The elder, in turn, already touched the lower or upper world – about to return, bearer of wisdom.

Likewise, dreams were not fantasies: they were journeys of the shadow soul to other worlds. A dream of falling could reveal imbalance; a dream of ascent, connection with the divine. Dreaming of a dark river or a dry tree signaled that something needed healing before the soul fragmented.

Among the Altai, Buryat, Tuvan, and Yakut peoples, the division of worlds also informed the spiritual calendar. Certain days were propitious for ascending – dates linked to the solstice, the full moon, the rise of energy. Other days required withdrawal – times when the portals of the underworld opened. Shamans consulted these cycles before performing rites of healing, hunting, or protection.

In some clans, it was believed that the soul could get lost between worlds. In such cases, the shaman was summoned to retrieve it – a journey requiring courage, purity, and deep knowledge of the cosmic tree. This journey, though symbolic, left real marks. A shaman descending into the underworld for many nights might fall ill. Some were said to age prematurely, as each crossing wore down the body. Others returned with new gifts – visions, clairvoyance, spontaneous healings. The border between worlds was always dangerous. But absolutely necessary.

At the center of this worldview lies a clear lesson: the universe is multiple, dynamic, interconnected. One cannot harm the earth without harming the sky. One cannot ignore the lower spirits without them manifesting disastrously. One cannot live in the middle world without looking up and down – because living in the middle world is walking between tensions, seeking balance, humility, listening.

Today, this wisdom echoes with urgency. The modern world, by detaching itself from the vertical axis of existence, plunged into imbalance. Forgot those above. Rejected those below. Inflated the human ego as master of reality. The result is a civilization orphaned from the World Tree: rootless, branchless, stuck to a dry trunk. Tengriism, with its ancestral clarity, offers a reminder: the worlds are still here. The sky still pulses. The underworld still breathes. And the middle can still be healed.

This possibility of healing begins with inner reconnection. Each individual carries within them a spark of the three worlds – an ancestral memory of the cosmic tree. Retaking this axis is, first and foremost, relearning to listen to the directions of being: the light calling us upward, the shadow inviting introspection, and the present summoning us to responsibility. The shaman, in this sense, is less a chosen one and more a mirror: his journey shows what each person, in their own measure, can tread. The challenge lies not just in crossing worlds, but in keeping the soul whole while doing so.

In daily life, this reconnection is expressed in simple yet powerful gestures: lighting a candle in silence, respecting nature's rhythm, sleeping attentive to dreams, treating seemingly inert things with reverence. These actions reweave the bridge between planes. The modern world need not imitate ancient rites, but can extract practical wisdom from them: perceiving that everything communicates, vibrates, responds. The universe is not an indifferent stage – it is a living tree pulsating with our conduct, choices, listening.

It is in this silent reunion with the world tree that the chance for regeneration resides. When we again recognize the sky not as an idea, but presence; the underworld not as threat, but space for transformation; and the middle world as sacred ground where everything intertwines, something within us begins to align. The world doesn't need to be different. It needs to be reinhabited with a different consciousness. Because, even when forgotten, the tree remains. And for those wishing to climb its branches or heal its roots, the drum still sounds.

Chapter 9
Celestial World

Above the rolling steppes, above the passing clouds, even above the eagles in flight, extends the celestial world – a plane of existence serene, luminous, unreachable by physical eyes, yet present at every moment in the spiritual consciousness of Tengriist peoples. This is not an empty, cold, mechanical sky, like the modern sky of astronomy, but a living, conscious space, filled with presences. At the heart of Tengriism, the celestial world is the dwelling place of benevolent gods, elevated ancestors, spirits guiding the universe's balance. It is origin and destination, cradle and judgment.

Tengri, Father Sky, is the supreme force permeating and sustaining this world. He is not one god among others, but the firmament itself – not in the physical sense, but as encompassing consciousness, eternally blue, eternally present. His domain is not of thrones or crowns, but of invisible order. Where there is harmony, there is Tengri. Where there is justice, there his will is manifest. He commands not with voice, but with wind. Dictates not, but inspires. And in the celestial world belonging to him, everything vibrates in consonance with his presence.

It is said that this upper world has layers – levels or floors reflecting different degrees of spiritual purity. In some traditions, there are seven heavens; in others, nine. This multiplicity is not simple spatial multiplication, but energetic gradation. In the lowest heaven dwell spirits still maintaining ties with the human world. They are recent ancestors, clan guardians, place protectors. As one ascends, older deities are found, personified cosmic principles, like Ulgen, Mergen, and Kayra. And at the highest point resides what cannot be described – the absolute purity of the Eternal Sky.

Ulgen, for example, is often cited as the great organizer of good. He is not the creator of everything, but the one who ensures the continuity of order. His role is to watch over humans honoring the laws of heaven, offering them protection and inspiration. It is he who sends shamans in dreams. It is he who observes rituals performed with sincerity. In some versions of the myth, it is Ulgen who shapes the destinies of souls ascending after death – assigning them dwellings in different heavens according to their degree of righteousness.

Mergen, another celestial spirit, is the archetype of wisdom and contemplation. His name means "the Insightful," "the Wise." He dwells in the heaven of intelligence, where pure thoughts flow like crystalline rivers. It is said that Mergen rides on white clouds, wielding a bow of light with which he shoots ideas at inspired humans. Poets, healers, prophets – all, at some point, receive an invisible arrow from Mergen. And when this happens, something changes: a verse emerges, a healing occurs, a just decision is made. Because the upper sky acts through signs, not words.

Kayra, in turn, is the primordial principle. Some confuse him with Tengri, others see him as his first son. In every narrative, he is the oldest of the celestials. Represents origin, the beginning before time. When the universe was still a cosmic egg, Kayra was the breath that made it crack. He has no form, color, or limit. He is pure presence. Many shamans report, in their deepest trances, having "touched" Kayra – not with senses, but with soul. They describe him as absolute silence, white light, an indescribable feeling of unity. After such an encounter, they are never the same.

These inhabitants of the celestial world do not live in a "paradise" in the Christian sense. They do not rest in idleness. They work. They watch. They observe humans with interest and compassion. Receive their prayers, respond with blessings or warnings. Sometimes, they manifest in natural phenomena: a cloud shaped like an animal, a rainbow appearing after a rite, a shooting star during an invocation. Everything is communication. Everything is presence.

Human souls, upon dying, do not automatically ascend to the celestial world. Merit, purification, recognition are needed. A soul might wander between worlds, or be welcomed by familiar spirits. But when it ascends to the heavens, it becomes an elevated *aruğ* – an ancestor who not only protects, but guides with deep wisdom. These souls do not forget the living. They guide them, inspire them, warn them in dreams. And above all, they witness. Nothing a human does escapes the eyes of heaven. Because, for the Tengriist, to live is to be under constant observation from the upper world – not as oppressive surveillance, but as loving, demanding, and just presence.

Therefore, before major decisions, one looks to the sky. Asks for Tengri's approval. Seeks a sign. The flight of a bird, the change of wind, the shape of a cloud. Everything can be an answer. And when the sign is given, one moves forward with courage. Because acting in tune with the sky is acting with truth. And whoever walks with the sky fears no fall.

In ceremonies, invoking the celestial world is common practice. The shaman raises hands, dances in spirals, sings in forgotten tongues. Meanwhile, those present observe the fire, await the breeze, listen to the drum. And, at some point, they feel: the veil has torn. Something descended. A presence filled the space. The invisible became almost palpable. In these moments, the middle world touches the upper world. And humans, even if for seconds, know they are part of something larger, eternal, sublime.

The celestial world is also remembered in songs, proverbs, and stories. Children learn early that "who deceives the tribe, will be forgotten by the heavens"; or that "honest words rise fast like smoke to Tengri." These sayings are not just folkloric morality. They are living reminders that the Sky sees, the Sky listens, the Sky responds.

Today, when many look up and see only space and stars, the Tengriist sees home, path, memory. Sees the reflection of what they will one day become again.

The sky is not an external mystery. It is a mirror of the soul. And the celestial world is not an ancient fantasy – it is a dimension of the now, accessible to the heart that knows how to listen, to the spirit that knows how to ascend.

The celestial world, beyond its grandeur, reveals a subtle pedagogy: everything coming from above descends not as imposition, but invitation. The sky demands not blind worship, but attunement. And this attunement is built with inner cultivation: attentive listening, integral word, gesture aligned with truth. Living under the sky is, therefore, a spiritual commitment to clarity, humility, and listening. Every impure thought, every dishonest action, obscures the bond with the upper plane. But every sincere repentance, every act of righteousness, rebuilds the bridge. It is not the rite that guarantees connection, but the coherence between thought, feeling, and action.

There is, in this elevated horizon, a kind of luminous solace. Knowing there are loving eyes above – not judging eyes, but witnesses of our effort – strengthens the walk. Because even in the deepest solitude, even when rites seem empty or dreams fall silent, there is still a presence. Tengri and the celestials respond not in the time of human anxiety, but in the cadence of eternity. Sometimes, the sought sign comes not in the wind, but in silence. And even this silence carries wisdom – a call to trust, persist, ascend with a light heart.

Therefore, honoring the celestial world is not just looking up with reverence, but living such that heaven can dwell within. When the human walks in harmony with the rhythms of soul and earth, when they do not betray what is sacred in themselves and others, the sky need no longer be invoked – it manifests. Not as spectacle, but serene presence. And in that instant, even amidst the struggles of the middle world, the soul recognizes: it is home.

Chapter 10
Underworld

In the hidden depths of reality, beneath the surface of the plains and below the apparent solidity of the earth, rests the underworld – a sphere of existence shrouded in shadow, silence, and mystery. For Tengriist peoples, this world is not an invention to frighten, but a palpable reality, integral to the triune structure of the cosmos. It is as necessary as the sky and the middle earth. It is the domain of the hidden, the unresolved, what needs transformation. And above all, it is the place where forgotten and repressed forces sleep – or stir.

The underworld, called by many names across the steppes of Central Asia, has its own logic, inhabitants, rules. In it, souls unable to ascend to the celestial world, whether due to imbalance or actions in life, find temporary dwelling. But it is not hell in the Western sense. It is not a place of eternal punishment, but of suspension. An in-between world, where the spirit learns, suffers, reconfigures itself – or perishes.

In this domain reigns a central figure: Erlik Khan. Known as the Lord of the Underworld, Erlik is not the "devil" of monotheisms. He is older than dualistic morality. Represents the power of containment, the necessary shadow, the guardian of the borders between life and death. According to some myths, Erlik was one of the first beings created, but his ambition led to his fall. Others say he was tasked by Tengri to guard the underworld, keeping there energies that could not roam freely in the cosmos.

Erlik is described as an entity of mutable appearance. Sometimes an old man with a dark face and long beard; other times, a somber warrior with eyes like incandescent coals. In all versions, he carries the weight of the threshold – his presence announces crisis, rupture, but also opportunity for change. He commands legions of tormented spirits, lesser demons, and confused souls. These beings, though feared, have a function: they test, challenge, reveal human weaknesses.

In the underworld, the landscape is an inverted mirror of earthly reality. There are mountains, rivers, cities, but everything is veiled in a dark hue, as if sunlight never reached those regions. The rivers are not of water, but of mists and laments. The forests are dense, where each tree guards a secret. Dwellings are caves carved into living rock. There, souls tread confusing paths, repeat mistakes, seek escape. Some find it. Others do not.

It was said that on certain nights, the doors of the underworld opened slightly. And the dreams of the living became vivid, laden with omens. It was at these moments that shamans took action. For one of the riskiest – and noblest – roles of the shaman was to descend into the underworld. In deep trance, guided by ancestral chants and rhythmic drum beats, he left his body and departed. The journey was not metaphorical. It was real. The shaman crossed stone portals, traversed the river of souls, faced cave guardians. All to recover something: a lost soul, a sick child, a clan's stolen luck.

These descents were not without dangers. Many shamans returned ill, exhausted, disturbed. Some did not return – their souls remained trapped, or they chose to stay as guardians. Therefore, a shaman's training included learning the names of underworld entities, their pleasures and aversions. A mistake in ritual, a poorly intoned chant, a poorly chosen offering, and the shaman could be spiritually devoured. The necessary courage was not heroic in the vulgar sense – it was existential. It was knowing that upon descending, one might never be the same again.

But not only shamans related to the underworld. Common people also knew of its presence. When someone suddenly fell ill, it was said their soul had been dragged below. When a herd mysteriously disappeared, Erlik's wrath was suspected. To prevent such misfortunes, appeasement rituals were performed. Dark-coated animals – black rams, black roosters – were sacrificed at the village thresholds. The spilled blood was a gesture of conciliation, a plea for Erlik not to cross his borders. To keep his eyes on the world below.

There were also thanksgiving ceremonies. When someone recovered from a serious illness, it was believed they had been rescued from the underworld's clutches. On these occasions, a feast was prepared. Not just for the living, but for the spirits. Dishes were left outdoors, near caves or ancient trees. Words were murmured to the "brothers below." Because respect maintained peace. And disrespecting the underworld was inviting ruin.

The underworld was also home to forgotten knowledge. Many myths told that spirits of ancient civilizations – those existing before known time – dwelt there. They were fallen masters, ancestral shamans, guardians of forbidden knowledge. In some rare rituals, shamans attempted to contact them. Not to learn tricks, but to obtain visions. These encounters were dangerous. But if successful, revealed hidden truths – about the world's origin, souls' destiny, the cycles governing everything.

In the modern world, the underworld continues to exist. Though many have forgotten it, it still pulses beneath everyone's feet. It manifests in identity crises, unexplained illnesses, disturbing dreams. It emerges when the soul strays from its center. And even without naming it, many feel its presence. Feel the invisible weight, the pull downward, the call to face what has been buried. The underworld demands confrontation. But also offers healing.

Therefore, Tengriism does not reject it. Does not build theologies to deny or banish it. On the contrary: recognizes its importance in the cosmic balance. Understands that every light casts a shadow. That every birth implies death. And that all growth requires descent. It is not about exalting darkness, but knowing how to coexist with it. To walk firmly on the ground, aware that it holds secrets – and that these secrets are part of the journey.

By understanding the underworld, the practitioner of Tengriism understands that no part of existence can be ignored. That reality is a tapestry of three threads – and cutting any one unravels the whole. The sky, the earth, and the underworld form a single body. And the human being, by living consciously, honors this totality.

Recognizing the underworld as a vital part of existence invites a more mature spirituality—one seeking not just ascent, but acceptance and integration. The shadow, in this context, is not enemy: it is mirror. Traversing it is diving into the deepest layers of the soul, where fears, guilts, and ancient pains rest awaiting listening. The underworld, thus, ceases to be merely the dwelling of the forgotten and becomes the territory of naked truth, where there are no masks, where everything denied cries out for name and form. No wonder so many healing rites require this contact: because only what is faced can truly be transformed.

In this descent, the role of the shaman and, by extension, any sincere seeker, is to become a bridge. It's not about bringing light to extinguish darkness, but learning to see within it. Myths about forgotten wisdoms underground are not distant metaphors—they are memories pointing to the power of the unconscious, the past, what modern reason rejects. And it is there, between rivers of lament and forests of silence, that the traveler finds not only answers, but recognition of their own complexity. For knowing the underworld is, ultimately, knowing oneself whole.

By including the underworld in life's tapestry, Tengriism offers us a radically whole vision of being.

Neither sky nor earth suffices alone. It is in the balance of the three worlds that the true path unfolds. A path requiring courage, lucidity, and humility—because living well is not avoiding the fall, but learning to rise after it. And whoever faces the dark with open eyes discovers that beneath the surface of pain pulses a silent force. A force redeeming not by denial, but by presence. And which, when embraced, transforms the abyss into root.

Chapter 11
Multiple Souls

Among the deepest mysteries of Tengriist spirituality is the concept that each human being is composed of more than one soul. This idea, which might seem strange to the Western mindset accustomed to thinking of the soul as a single, indivisible entity, is actually one of the most sophisticated expressions of spiritual psychology developed by the Turco-Mongol and Siberian peoples. It is not fragmentary mythology, but an integral vision of existence, where the being is multiple by essence, and each aspect of the soul fulfills a distinct function in the great tapestry of life.

This plur-substantia conception of the soul is deeply rooted in the nomadic experience. For the ancients of the steppes and taigas, the human being was not just flesh animated by an immaterial breath. It was a bundle of forces, a set of presences coexisting in precarious balance. Losing this balance meant falling ill. Losing a part of the soul could mean going mad, wasting away, or dying. Retrieving it was a shaman's most sacred mission.

The first of these souls, generally called *nefes* (from Turkish, meaning "breath"), corresponds to the vital breath. It is what animates the body, makes the blood circulate, eyes shine, skin warm. It enters the body with the newborn's first breath and departs with the last. It is intimately linked to respiration, heat, and life's movement. It is the most sensitive to changes in the physical world. A strong fright, sudden pain, high fever can affect it profoundly. If the *nefes* weakens, the body withers. If it departs, death ensues.

The second soul, more subtle and complex, is the so-called *shadow soul*, also known as the *free soul*. This is the part of the being that can temporarily detach from the body – in dreams, trances, intense spiritual experiences. It is seen as a traveler. It is through it that shamans explore invisible worlds. It is through it that humans have visions, encounters with spirits, memories of past lives. During the night, it is this soul that frees itself and roams other planes. If it gets lost or kidnapped, the body sleeps but does not dream. The spirit remains empty, and the person may wake up apathetic, disoriented, ill.

There is also the *sülde*, known among Mongols as the soul of personality. It is this soul that holds an individual's unique traits – temperament, courage, loyalty. It is the spark maintaining the sense of identity and purpose. It is believed that great warriors and leaders had an especially strong *sülde*. After death, this soul could remain as a clan's protective spirit, linked to personal objects, weapons, tents, banners. Therefore, *sülde* were often invoked in times of war or crisis, as inspiring forces.

Some peoples, like the Samoyeds and Altaians, speak of a fourth soul – related to luck, destiny, divine protection. This soul is tenuous as mist, difficult to detect, but essential. When present and whole, the person seems to live under a favorable star: paths open, dangers divert, endeavors prosper. When absent or wounded, life becomes full of inexplicable obstacles, as if the universe were in opposition. This soul could be transferred, gifted, or weakened by envy, magic, or curses.

In some traditions, there is even talk of a fifth soul – the ancestral soul. It would be the living memory of previous generations, present in each individual as an invisible thread linking them to their ancestors. This soul would be responsible for the sense of belonging, the intuition of being part of a lineage, a story larger than the ego. When this soul manifests, the person feels compelled to repeat ancient gestures, honor elders, protect traditional knowledge. The loss of this soul generates alienation, cultural disorientation, rupture.

These multiple souls, though interconnected, are distinct in nature and function. Each responds to different stimuli, inhabits different layers of being. And each requires specific care. Protecting the *nefes* means keeping the body strong and healthy. Cultivating the *free soul* involves dreaming, creating, meditating. Nourishing the *sülde* is acting with honor, keeping promises, respecting oneself. Guarding the soul of luck means avoiding envy, being envied, and staying in harmony with the universe's rhythms. Honoring the ancestral soul is remembering, thanking, continuing.

The shaman, in this context, is first and foremost a healer of souls. When someone falls ill, he asks not only about physical symptoms. He asks if the person had nightmares, if they feel "empty," if they have heard their inner voice. Often, the diagnosis is that one of the souls has been lost – frightened by trauma, seduced by a deceitful spirit, imprisoned in another plane. The ritual, then, is a journey to recover that soul. The shaman sings, dances, fights, cries, until the lost part reintegrates with the whole.

Soul loss is a central concept in Tengriism. Not as a poetic metaphor, but as a real phenomenon. Very frightened children, women after childbirth, men returning from wars—all could suffer this rupture. And there were specific rituals for each case. The soul was called by name, invited back, caressed with herb smoke, fed with milk or blood. Sometimes, a loved one needed to call for it. Because love has the power to reunite what fear fragmented.

This ancestral wisdom echoes in modern times with unexpected force. In an era marked by psychic illnesses, identity crises, loss of meaning, the notion of multiple souls offers a key. Depression could be, through the eyes of Tengriism, a free soul that has strayed. Anxiety could be the soul of destiny out of balance. Personality disorders might indicate a broken *sülde*. The remedy, then, lies not just in pharmaceuticals, but in rituals of reconnection: with the earth, ancestors, the sky.

The recognition of inner multiplicity also challenges the rigid boundaries between self and world. If my free soul travels, it can encounter other souls, in other times. If my *nefes* harmonizes with the wind, then the wind participates in my life. If my ancestral soul carries my people's history, then my life is a continuation, not a beginning. This view dissolves modern individualism and proposes an ecology of the soul – where every inner gesture reverberates in the universe, and every external event invites integration.

In Tengriism, full health is not the absence of disease, but harmony among the souls. When all are present, clean, nourished, the human being flourishes. Their eyes shine. Their word carries weight. Their path aligns with the forces of sky and earth. They need no commandments, because they feel internally what is just. Their ethics arise from the fullness of their parts. And their joy, from the awareness of being whole.

The multiplicity of souls, as proposed by Tengriism, also suggests a spiritual education extending beyond simple faith or doctrine. It implies intimate self-knowledge, sensitive listening to inner voices, and commitment to the subtler rhythms of being. In this context, living becomes an act of constant tuning between the soul's diverse dimensions—like a musician adjusting their instrument before playing, the human needs to recognize the strings vibrating within. Every emotion, intuition, impulse arising is seen not as chance or whim, but as a manifestation of one of these souls in its own language, asking for attention, balance, or healing.

At the same time, this spiritual model demands a communal view of existence. If parts of our soul can be affected by others' words, actions, even thoughts, then we are co-responsible for each other. The health of a clan, village, society depends on the mutual care of the souls living there. In this web, the shaman's role is not just that of an individual healer, but a harmonizer of the collective. He acts as a bridge between worlds and between people, restoring bonds, reanimating what was dispersed. The community, in turn, recognizes the value of this role not out of superstition, but direct experience: when one soul returns, everyone breathes easier.

Each being is, then, a living constellation, in constant dance with the invisible. Perceiving oneself thus transforms how one faces suffering, celebrates joy, and traverses life. There is no rush to "solve" what hurts, but patience in listening to what each pain reveals about souls in misalignment. At the same time, ecstasy is not feared, for it is understood there are moments when the free soul touches the divine. Living, in this light, is both mystery and learning: an invitation to walk whole, even when in pieces, trusting there is wisdom in each fragment and that the sky always listens.

Chapter 12
Shaman Mediator

Between the veils separating the visible world from invisible dimensions, there is a figure who walks with feet on the earth and eyes on the sky, who listens to the murmur of winds and understands the language of waters, who dialogues with the dead and heals the living. This figure is the shaman – the mediator par excellence of Tengriism. He is not priest, orator, messiah. He is a living bridge between worlds. His craft is not teaching truths, but restoring connections. He is guide, healer, spiritual warrior, tribal counselor, and ally of spirits. In the vastness of the steppe, where religion is not confined to temples but pulses in every mountain, river, or tree, the shaman is the axis keeping the community attuned to the universe's rhythms.

His birth is not always desired. Many are chosen, they do not choose. The call comes as illness, visions, recurring dreams, inexplicable misfortunes. When a person begins hearing voices no one else hears, seeing animals speak, or feeling pains doctors cannot explain, the elders know: perhaps Tengri has placed upon him the burden and gift of *kamlık*, the shamanic path. This call is usually confirmed by an older shaman who recognizes the signs. The initiation then begins – and it is rigorous. Involves isolation, fasts, physical and spiritual trials. The candidate must symbolically die to the common world and be reborn as a mediator. In certain traditions, it is said the future shaman's spirit is literally dismembered by otherworldly entities and then reconstituted with crystal bones and flesh of fire. This "ritual death" is a condition for him to enter and exit worlds without being destroyed. He who has not been broken cannot heal the broken.

Once recognized as a shaman, the individual receives a new name – often revealed in a dream or transmitted by a protective spirit. He begins wearing specific attire during rituals: tunics with medals, mirrors, bells, animal skins. Each adornment has meaning. Mirrors reflect and ward off evil spirits. Skins evoke the shaman's allies – wolves, eagles, bears. Bells announce his passage between worlds. The drum is his horse. With it, the shaman rides through heavens and abysses.

The drum, indeed, is inseparable from the shaman. Crafted from sacred wood and consecrated hide, it is more than an instrument – it is a spirit itself. The rhythmic, deep, pulsating sound induces trance, alters consciousness, opens invisible portals. By playing it, the shaman enters another state of perception. His eyes roll back, voice changes, movements become fluid and unpredictable. In this state, he can ascend to the celestial world for guidance, or descend to the underworld to free trapped souls.

Each journey is unique. No trance is like another. Sometimes, the shaman finds a lost child needing guidance back to the body. Other times, faces vengeful spirits demanding reparations. On some occasions, dialogues with ancestors to understand the reason for a curse or the origin of an illness. These encounters are symbolic, yes, but also concrete. The shaman experiences them as living realities. He returns with information, guidance, blessings, or warnings. His truth results from direct experience, not doctrine.

In the tribe's daily life, the shaman is not just invoked in extreme situations. He is part of life. People consult him before a hunt, a journey, a marriage. He interprets omens, analyzes animal behavior, reads sky signs. He is called to bless a child's birth or console family members facing death. He ensures the deceased's soul reaches the ancestral world safely. In some cultures, this role is known as psychopomp – conductor of souls.

But the shaman also heals. And heals profoundly. When illness strikes someone, and remedies fail, the shaman is called. He investigates the spiritual origin of the ailment: was it a lost soul? An offended forest spirit? A forgotten ancestor? A broken pact? Based on this, prescribes a ritual: smoke baths, offerings, dances, prayers. Sometimes, he extracts "magical" objects from the sick body – stones, thorns, invisible insects. Sometimes, just sings. And healing happens. Not because he is a miracle worker, but because he knows how to restore interrupted flow.

The shaman's relationship with spirits is based on mutual respect. He does not command them. He negotiates. Learns their names, tastes, moods. Has auxiliary spirits – called *ongon* – accompanying him on journeys. Some are his ancestors, others nature entities. These spirits do not possess him, but protect him. When a shaman enters deep trance, often it is an *ongon* who speaks, gives advice, makes prophecies. The people listen attentively. Know that a wisdom not human speaks there.

It is important to note that in classic Tengriism there is no organized religious institution. No hierarchy of priests, no fixed temples. Each shaman is autonomous, and his legitimacy comes from effectiveness. If he heals, guides, sees the invisible, then he is respected. Otherwise, loses the people's trust. This gives the shaman enormous responsibility. Cannot lie, nor manipulate. His life is transparent, because his soul is exposed to the heavens' gaze. And he knows Tengri does not tolerate imposture.

Women can also be shamans – they are the *udgan* among Mongols. They possess particular gifts, often more linked to healing, spiritual motherhood, mediation with female and earth spirits. In some traditions, *udgan* are seen as capable of reaching even deeper levels of trance. Their songs are sweet, yet powerful. When entering altered states, their voice sounds like Mother Earth's. And those who hear them feel healed just by the sound.

Today, even in urban and globalized contexts, shamans continue to exist. Many operate in cities, serving people seeking meaning, healing, reconnection. Some have adapted their rituals, using candles, incense, modern drums. But the principle is the same: connecting the human being to the invisible forces sustaining them.

In regions like Tuva, Buryatia, Yakutia, and Mongolia, there are shaman federations, initiation schools, spiritual congresses. Ancient knowledge finds new ways to manifest, but the essence remains intact.

Observing the continuity of shamanic practice today, one perceives that the modern shaman, despite navigating urban environments and dealing with contemporary issues, remains faithful to his ancestral function: restoring the broken link between humans and the invisible planes of existence. Pains have changed form, but not essence. If previously evils came from the forest or clan, today they come from information overload, disconnection from the body, absence of roots. The shaman recognizes these new soul landscapes, but still treads the same subtle paths to bring healing. He understands that, even amidst city concrete, the spirit continues asking for space to breathe.

Beyond individual healing, today's shaman also acts as guardian of an ancestral memory at risk of erasure. By keeping chants, rituals, myths, and sacred gestures alive, he preserves not just a tradition, but a way of living and perceiving the world. In a time of rupture, his presence is a reminder that there are wisdoms not bending to linear time, speaking of cycles, deep listening, integration. He is not there to compete with science or established religions, but to remind that there are other ways of knowing – ways passing through the body, dream, silence.

Thus, the shaman remains an essential figure in any time: one who fears not the invisible, dives into shadows to light small flames, walks between worlds with humility and firmness. His existence invites a re-education of the gaze – not to see more, but to see better. Listening to his drums and stories, we are led to recognize that true healing is not erasing pain, but reintegrating what was separated. And in this, the shaman, with his mirrors, bells, and chants, continues being a bridge: between past and future, visible and invisible, human being and all that is.

Chapter 13
Sacred Rituals

On the wind-swept steppes, under the immense and silent sky, the nomadic people built no stone temples nor erected cathedrals – but every mountain, every tree, every lit fire was a living altar. At the heart of Tengriism, sacred rituals are the thread sewing together the worlds: sky, earth, underworld, and human spirit. They are not ceremonies to impress, nor acts of submission to a distant deity. They are gestures of communion. Offices of balance. Dialogues with the invisible forces sustaining existence.

From the dawn of a new day to the great cycles of the year, Tengriism expresses itself in rituals. They vary from clan to clan, people to people, but share a structure: offering, invocation, presence, silence. The material is simple – milk, smoke, meat, fire, stone – but the intention is profound. Ritual action is always relational: not done "for" the gods, but "with" them. Like sharing a meal with an ancient relative, a close spirit.

The first ritual, and perhaps the most daily, is the offering to the sky upon awakening. In the first light of morning, especially in traditional families, a little milk is poured upwards. Not as superstition, but as thanksgiving. Milk, the herd's essence, is shared life. The gesture is accompanied by words – sometimes murmured, sometimes sung. "Father Sky, receive our day. Guide our steps. Protect our home." It is a prayer without a book, but with soul. There is no ceremony more sincere than this morning offering.

Other rituals occur around the domestic fire, which is itself a spirit. Fire, for Tengriism, is a living being. Possesses mood, memory, wisdom. Must be lit with respect, fed sparingly, and never insulted with coarse words. Each morning, the first fire is greeted. During meals, a piece is thrown into the fire – "for the spirits." On nights of decision or illness, one sings to the fire. It is the center of the home, the link to ancestors, the invisible guardian. Garbage is not thrown into the fire. It is not extinguished with anger. It listens.

Animal sacrifice, present in many traditions, is also part of Tengriist rituals – but with important distinctions. One does not kill for killing's sake. The animal's life is respected. Before the cut, there is prayer. The family head or shaman asks permission from the animal's spirit, thanks Mother Earth, and offers the life to the Sky. On rare occasions, a white horse is sacrificed to Tengri – an extremely rare gesture, reserved for extreme events. The horse, the nomad's companion, is seen as an intermediary between worlds. Its ritual death is a journey offered to the spiritual world.

Another central ritual is the *ovoo tahilga*, performed at stone mounds – the *ovoo* – scattered across hills. These mounds are natural altars, passage markers, points of contact with earth and sky spirits. When passing an *ovoo*, it is customary to walk around it three times clockwise and leave an offering: a stone, a blue scarf, a little milk, vodka, or tobacco. Each gesture is a greeting, a request, a renewal of alliance with the place's invisible guardians. Climbing a hill for this purpose is more than hiking – it is spiritual ascent.

In the year's great celebrations, rituals become collective. At the summer solstice, for example, outdoor festivities are held. Families gather, light bonfires, dance, sing. A shaman leads the invocation to benevolent spirits, thanks Tengri for light, harvest, life. At this moment, the entire community is one soul. Children learn the chants. Elders repeat the stories. Young people renew their identity. It is rite, festival, mirror of cosmic order reflected in the social body.

When there is illness, ritual transforms into healing. The shaman consults spirits, prepares the space – it could be a tent, clearing, house. The drum begins to sound. Fire is lit with chosen wood. The patient is purified with juniper or artemisia smoke. The shaman dances, enters trance, dialogues with the hidden world. The ritual can last hours, sometimes all night. The community watches in silence or participates with clapping, chants, cries. If the lost soul returns, the patient opens eyes. Cries. Breathes. Smiles. The ritual fulfilled its purpose.

There are also rites of passage – birth, puberty, marriage, death. Birth is celebrated with blessings from Mother Earth and Umay, goddess protector of children. Talismans are placed in the cradle, soft chants are sung, and fire is kept lit to ward off hostile spirits. Puberty, especially among boys, is marked by small rites of courage: riding a wild horse, hunting with elders, spending a night alone under the sky. Marriage is a union not just between two people, but two lineages, two spiritual houses. The ritual is accompanied by dances, libations, and vows before the sky.

Death, perhaps the most solemn rite, is treated with reverence and calm. The body is washed, anointed, dressed in its best clothes. Fire is kept alive in the house. Chants are sung to guide the soul. The shaman may accompany the crossing, ensuring the soul reaches the right place among ancestors. In the following days, offerings of food and drink are made – not because the dead eat, but because the gesture feeds the link between worlds. The soul, now free, can visit the living, protect descendants, send signs in dreams.

In all these practices, a notable absence of dogmatic rigidity is observed. Tengriist rituals do not obey sacred books. They are not followed out of fear of punishment, but desire for connection. Spirituality expresses itself in gesture, song, the silence between words. Each clan, each family, adapts rituals to its way of life, territory, needs. There is no orthodoxy. There is coherence with life. And this coherence is measured by collective well-being, harmony with nature, the felt presence of spirits.

In modern times, many of these rituals have resurfaced. No longer as folkloric relics, but as living spiritual practices. In Mongolia, it's common to see young people climbing mountains to offer vodka to Tengri. In Kazakhstan, traditional festivals include fire rites and prayers to ancestors. In Yakutia, the Yhyakh festival has been vigorously revived, combining ancient dances, sky chants, and shamanic blessings. Even in urban environments, small altars with stones, fabrics, and incense appear on apartment balconies. The ritual adapts. And the soul feels at home.

Tengriism, with its holistic worldview, teaches that there is no separation between sacred and mundane. Cooking can be ritual. Caring for animals can be offering. Observing the night sky can be prayer. What matters is not formalism, but intention. Where there is presence, respect, openness, there is ritual. And where there is ritual, there is connection. And where there is connection, there is healing.

The continuity of Tengriist rituals in the present shows that their essence lies not in the objects used or places where they occur, but in the quality of the bond they establish. Amidst the hurried pace of contemporary life, they offer a return to circular time, to meaningful gesture, to full attention. Even if the landscape changes and symbols transform, the ritual's spirit remains: creating a fissure in the everyday through which the invisible can breathe. By lighting a candle, touching the drum, leaving an offering of milk, the practitioner reweaves the bridge between human and cosmos, recalling that life is not just what is seen, but also everything pulsating behind the veil of the visible.

These rituals, through their malleability and depth, reveal a spirituality of listening and reciprocity. It's not about dominating the spiritual world, but relating to it, with humility and reverence. Each ritual gesture carries the weight of tradition and the lightness of the present. By involving body, voice, memory, and intention, the rite becomes complete. It educates the heart, realigns thought, and strengthens the sense of belonging. Children grow knowing the sky deserves respect, fire is alive, the listened-to stone responds. It is not blind faith, but sensitive learning, where each natural element becomes a master.

The true legacy of Tengriism's sacred rituals is not just cultural or spiritual, but existential. They remind that the human is not above nature, but within it, as one voice in the great cosmic song. When this song is sung with the whole body, present soul, and open hands, it heals – not as miracle, but reconnection. And this is a ritual's greatest gift: not changing the world around, but allowing the world within us to realign with sky, earth, and all living between them.

Chapter 14
Shamanic Healing

The soul, in the Tengriist universe, does not fall ill in silence. When unbalanced, it speaks – through the body, mood, destiny that clouds over. For the nomadic peoples of the steppe and taiga, illness was not just a physiological accident, but a sign of rupture between the human being and the visible and invisible worlds. Healing, therefore, was not a mechanical operation, but a spiritual journey. And the healer, par excellence, was the shaman. His drum was not an instrument of spectacle, but a scalpel of the soul. His words were not metaphors, but living formulas. He treated not symptoms, but causes. Not just what hurt, but what was absent. Shamanic healing was reconnection.

To fully understand how this healing occurs, it is necessary to abandon the modern separation between mind, body, and spirit. In Tengriism, everything is interconnected: the individual's health depends on alignment with nature, ancestors, and the multiple souls composing their existence. Illness can arise from various spiritual causes: soul loss (very common), intrusion of a malevolent spirit, breaking a natural taboo, or even energetic imbalance generated by prolonged, undigested emotions – like envy, fear, resentment. The shaman is called not just when all else fails, but when it is perceived that the visible world cannot account for the explanation.

The process begins with listening. The shaman, when sought, does not formulate diagnoses in the technical sense of modern medicine. He observes, listens to the voice's timbre, how eyes move, what is said, and especially, what is not said. Sometimes he asks no questions. Just plays his drum, closes eyes, attunes to auxiliary spirits. Asks them what happened. And the spirits respond – through images, sounds, sensations. On other occasions, a dream reveals the illness's origin. Or an animal's behavior, or the wind blowing differently that morning.

When the spiritual cause is identified, the healing ritual is prepared. It can be simple or elaborate, depending on the case's severity. Sometimes, a juniper smoke bath suffices to disperse an intruding spirit. Other times, long nights of chants, dances, offerings, and confrontations are needed. In many cases, the shaman enters a trance and travels spiritually to the underworld, where the patient's soul might be trapped. On this journey, he negotiates with underworld guardians, offers gifts, chants sacred names, until freeing the soul. When it returns, the patient, previously apathetic and distant, awakens as from a long sleep. Opens eyes. Breathes deeply. Cries.

Another common method is spiritual suction. The shaman identifies the body point where the intrusion lodged – it could be a spell, an evil spirit, or an ethereal "object" – and sucks with his mouth. Then spits into the fire. The sound heard upon falling can signal the evil was burned. Often, the shaman presents the removed object: a dark stone, a tiny bone, an invisible worm. The gesture is symbolic, but no less effective. Because the patient feels light. Says the weight is gone. That the knot loosened.

There are also soul retrieval rituals. When part of the soul is lost – whether through trauma, fright, or grief – it can wander, forget to return. The shaman, then, calls for it. Three times, in a firm, melodious voice, says the soul's name. Beckons with offerings, reminds it who it is, where it lives, who loves it. The soul, sensitized, returns. Upon returning, the patient's gaze changes. A spark rekindles. Shamans say that when the soul returns, the body smiles – even in silence.

Shamanic healings also involve natural elements: stones, plants, water, fire. The shaman knows herbs that cleanse, warm, numb, awaken. Knows where the root grows that wards off fear. Knows to burn the leaf that repels bad winds. But nothing is used without spiritual consent. Before harvesting, the shaman asks the plant's permission. Gives thanks. Leaves something in return – a strand of hair, a little milk, a stone. Healing, in Tengriism, is always reciprocal. Nothing is taken without giving.

There are also treatments with water: baths in sacred rivers, dips in specific springs, or even washing with water consecrated by chants. Water, symbol of life and flow, is a vehicle of purification. It carries away what is old, stagnant, corrupted. In some traditions, the patient must fast before receiving the water. In others, must undergo trials – like facing darkness, listening without speaking, enduring cold – to demonstrate to the soul their willingness to heal.

In the most severe cases, healing depends on the entire clan. The shaman summons everyone. The ritual becomes collective. Everyone claps, chants refrains, feeds the fire. It's not just about helping the sick. It's about rebalancing the community. Because one person's illness can reflect the illness of the whole. And true healing is that which reaches everyone. Therefore, even today, many rituals are done in groups. Even in cities, even among strangers. Because when one soul heals, all rejoice.

There are cases where healing does not occur. The soul is ready to depart. The shaman, then, does not force. His role becomes another: guiding. Preparing the spirit for the journey. Ensuring the dead find the right path. Consoling the living. Showing that death is not end, but transition. In many cases, the shaman's presence at the moment of death is more important than any treatment. Because he sings to the detaching soul. And the soul, hearing its name sung, crosses over serenely.

In modern times, shamanic healing remains alive. In alternative hospitals, spiritual retreats, urban indigenous communities. The drum continues sounding. Smoke continues rising. The soul continues being called. Many seek it as a last hope. Others, as a first choice. Some see it as superstition. But there are also those who witness inexplicable healings. Who feel the soul return. Who see the sparkle reborn in eyes. And that suffices.

The persistence of shamanic healing in the contemporary world reveals an ancestral need resurfacing in new guises: reconnecting the human being with what was lost—not only on the spiritual plane, but also the symbolic, emotional, relational. Even facing technological medicine, with its precise diagnoses and sophisticated therapies, a void remains untouched. Shamanic healing does not compete with science; it acts where exams cannot reach: in the terrain of the invisible, silenced memory, trauma still echoing. It does not deny pain, but listens to it. And by listening, invites the soul to return to itself.

This deep, sacred listening is perhaps the shaman's greatest gift. He heals not by imposition, but presence. His strength lies in total availability to the spiritual world, and skill in deciphering the language of winds, stones, eyes suffering silently. The healing he offers is not uniform, nor predictable. Each patient is a universe. Each soul, a mystery. Therefore, the shaman applies no techniques—he surrenders to the rite like entering a dark forest, confident he will be guided. And when returns, brings not just relief, but meaning. Pain, even when persisting, is no longer mute. And that transforms.

True healing, according to Tengriist shamanism, lies not just in "eliminating" disease, but restoring life's flow. When this flow returns, even death can be received peacefully. Because the soul, then, is no longer lost, nor fragmented—it is whole, self-aware, connected to the sacred web involving all things. The shaman, with drum and song, continues being the conductor of this return. And as long as there are souls seeking home, his path will never cease.

Chapter 15
Totems and Symbols

The rolling steppes, the snowy peaks of the Altai, and the vast deserts of Central Asia are landscapes where ancient winds whisper secrets not forgotten, only dormant. Within these lands, nomadic peoples built no stone temples, but erected their spirituality on the invisible lines uniting man, animal, sky, and earth. And to give form to this spiritual universe, they created symbols – living images, bearers of power. The totems and symbols of Tengriism are not just decorative emblems or tribal marks: they are condensations of wisdom, bridges between worlds, mirrors of the collective soul.

The totem, in the Tengriist context, is more than a sacred figure. It is a living ancestor, a spiritual presence guiding and protecting. Each clan, tribe, family group could have its totemic animal – a being with which it shared virtues, stories, destiny. Wolves, for example, occupy a central place in many founding myths. For the ancient Turks, the Bozkurt, the grey wolf, was the ancestral guide leading them through darkness to a new valley of hope. The myth of Asena, the she-wolf who originated Turkic lineages, symbolizes this deep union between human and animal. Wolves were not just feared or admired: they were spiritual brothers. When they howled at night, it was heard as a call of blood, a reminder of origins. A warrior carrying the wolf on his banner or tattooed on his body did not just imitate its courage – he evoked the protection of the totemic spirit that had watched over his people for generations. The wolf was cunning, loyal to the group, fast, and silent – qualities desired by all living by constant movement and vigilance in wild lands.

Other equally powerful totems included the deer, eagle, bear, and horse. The deer, graceful and vigilant, was seen as a messenger of the gods and guide of souls. In some tales, it is the deer appearing to the shaman in a dream and leading him through the World Tree. The eagle, with its sharp vision and majestic flight, represented the all-seeing spirit, the bridge between high and low. It was a symbol of direct connection with Tengri. The bear, in turn, was untamed strength, the guardian of forests. Among Siberian and Altaic peoples, the bear is often considered the primordial ancestor, protector of children, and healer. The horse, the nomad's inseparable companion, is more than a mount – it is a mediator between worlds, transport of souls, symbol of freedom and fidelity.

These totems lived not only in stories: they were present in everyday objects. They were carved on warriors' bows, embroidered on ceremonial robes, painted on shamanic drums. Shamanic art, incidentally, is pure symbolic language. Each line, spiral, dot on the drum hide represents a level of reality, a sacred direction, a guardian spirit. The drum itself is a microcosm: its circular rim represents the middle world; its flat surface, the visible sky; the hide bottom, the lower world. When the shaman plays the drum, he activates all planes of existence.

In Tengriist symbology, certain visual elements appear repeatedly and with great force: the sun, moon, tree, and circle. The sun – Gun Ana, Mother Sun – is life, warmth, blessing. The moon – Ay Ata, Father Moon – is nocturnal protection, balance, intuition. Both are considered celestial deities and appear in chants, banners, pendants. The flag of Kyrgyzstan, for example, features a stylized sun with forty rays, a direct reference to Tengriist cosmology.

The world tree, present at the center of many shamanic drawings, is the axis connecting the three worlds: its roots touch the underworld, its trunk traverses the middle world, and its crown reaches the sky. The circle, finally, represents totality, the cycle of life, the sky's eternity. It is a recurring symbol in yurt ornaments, drums, and jewelry. The round skylight at the top of tents – the Mongolian *töönö* – is a symbol in itself. It is where the sacred fire's smoke rises. Where the sky is seen. Where spirits enter. The *töönö* is the house's pupil, the eye connecting home to firmament. During rituals, the shaman looks at it when seeking signs from the sky. Some traditions say the souls of the dead exit through it to reach the celestial world. Therefore, the *töönö* is never covered at certain times of day.

With the modern revival of Tengriism, new symbols began to be created, based on ancient traditions. One of the most widespread is the emblem uniting the runic script for "Tengri," the drawing of the yurt opening, and the shape of the shamanic drum. This triple symbol appears on amulets, tattoos, and banners of contemporary Tengriist movements. It summarizes, in a single image, the three pillars of ancestral spirituality: sky, home, and spiritual path.

Colors also have deep meaning. Blue – especially turquoise blue – is the color of the sky, serenity, truth. It was used on shamans' sashes, tribal banners, ceremonial clothes. It's common to see blue scarves tied to sacred trees or over *ovoo*. White represents purity, benevolence, luminous spirits – the so-called "white Tengri." Black is associated with "black Tengri," severe spirits or those of the underworld, who are also respected, though feared. Red can represent life, blood, vital force. Each color, in each context, is silent prayer.

Certain objects became living symbols. The shaman's drum, for example, is a portable altar. The staff with bells, used to ward off negative spirits. The mirror attached to clothing – not for vanity, but magical protection. Amulets with animal eyes, specific stones, carved bones – all these are fragments of a spiritual alphabet that has resisted millennia. A symbol, for Tengriism, is not dead thing: it is condensed spirit. A wooden wolf can contain the memory of an entire clan. An eagle drawn on a shield can evoke the courage of past generations.

The transmission of these symbols occurs orally and visually. Children learn their forms, stories, uses early on. No books needed: knowledge is in chants, ornaments, elders' hands. By embroidering a cape with the sun symbol, a grandmother teaches about the light that never ceases. By carving a deer on a staff, a grandfather reminds that the spirit walks with the grandson. This is how symbolism is not lost. It lives. Circulates. Is reborn.

Even today, in urban contexts, these symbols find space. Young Turks tattoo the symbol of Tengri on their arms. Mongols hang miniature *ovoo* from car rearview mirrors. In contemporary ceremonies, new objects are consecrated as totemic: cameras for modern shamans recording the invisible; microphones used in rituals broadcast live online. The symbol adapts, without losing its soul. Because what makes it sacred is not the external form, but the intention and reverence animating it.

The totems and symbols of Tengriism, therefore, are not ornaments of a distant past. They are paths to the invisible. Bridges between ancestral and contemporary. Reminders that there is a greater order, a presence watching, a meaning escaping cold logic. In times of forgetfulness, they are roots. In times of confusion, they are compasses. In times of inner exile, they are home.

This symbolic potency is not limited to representing the sacred; it summons it, makes it present. Each totem, trace, color awakens in the individual and community a dormant memory, a call to something transcending the immediate. Tengriist symbols are not passive – they act, open inner portals, reorganize the intimate world. Observing the figure of a carved wolf is not just seeing art: it is touching, with eyes, the spirit that protects, the narrative that sustains, the identity that anchors. Thus, the symbol ceases to be mere image and becomes experience, a way of participating in invisible reality.

This participation is not abstract. It occurs in daily gestures, choices, spiritual alliances each person forms by bearing or evoking a symbol. Choosing to carry the sky's blue or the shaman's mirror is also assuming a stance before the world – of search, listening, responsibility. Symbols shape action, because they remind the bearer who they are and to which lineage of wisdom they belong. They are forms educating silently, whispering in daily life: "remember what inhabits you." And, in this sense, totems are not just outside – they are inside, latent, ready to be awakened.

That is why, even in a time when everything seems disposable and ephemeral, Tengriist symbols remain alive. They resist because they speak directly to the soul, needing no translation. Their strength lies in simplicity traversing time, in beauty still reverberating in the hands of those who draw, embroider, or erect an *ovoo* atop a hill. Each symbol is an invitation to reunion – with ancestors, nature, one's own spirit. And where there is reunion, there is path. And where there is path, even in the most arid landscapes, the soul finds direction.

Chapter 16
Sacred Sites

In a world where the landscape is more than backdrop, where every peak holds a spirit, every river has a voice, and every clearing hides a presence, the concept of sacred site gains a density beyond metaphor. In Tengriism, places are not just geographical spaces – they are beings. Ancient, conscious beings that breathe and observe. Each mountain, spring, singular tree is a living entity participating in the spiritual network linking Sky, Earth, and human being. Sacred sites are not arbitrarily chosen: they reveal themselves. And the ancients knew how to listen to them.

What defines a place's sacredness, then, is not human construction upon it, but its intrinsic nature. A solitary mountain on the horizon can become the point where sky touches earth. A clear spring can be the mouth through which Mother Earth whispers. And when humans recognize these points, they do not dominate them – they venerate them. Respect is expressed not in destruction or exploitation, but in silence, offering, attentive presence.

In Mongolia, one such sacred mountain is Burkhan Khaldun, located in Khentii province. Its name, translatable as "Sacred Mountain of God," is intertwined with the most symbolic history of the Mongol people: Genghis Khan, according to legends, was born there and prayed there countless times. He himself supposedly declared the mountain guardian of his lineage and sought Tengri's aid there before his great campaigns. Since then, Burkhan Khaldun is not just a geographical landmark, but a spiritual pillar. Mongols still climb its slopes on pilgrimage today, not for tourism, but to listen to ancestral echoes and pay tribute to the Sky.

Another revered peak is Khan Tengri, situated between Kazakhstan and Kyrgyzstan. Its name already denotes its nature: "Khan of the Sky" or "Celestial Lord." It is one of the highest mountains in the Tian Shan range and, due to its perfect pyramidal shape and eternal snow, has been identified since antiquity as the dwelling of higher beings. Peoples living nearby never climbed its summits without ceremonial purpose. Winds there are considered messengers. And when fog covers the summit, it is said Tengri is in council with spirits.

But not only great mountains possess sacredness. Many sacred sites are modest in appearance: a tree grown isolated in the steppe's middle, a cave hidden among rocks, a circular lake with still waters. What makes them special is not grandeur, but signs. The presence of animals not seen elsewhere. Anomalous wind behavior. The feeling that something there is watching, testing, waiting.

To mark these power points, nomadic peoples created *ovoo* (in Mongolian) or *oboo* (in Turkic). These are mounds of stones or wood erected at specific points – hilltops, mountain passes, crossroads. Each *ovoo* is an open-air altar. Offerings are deposited there: stones brought from afar, pieces of turquoise-blue fabric, bottles of vodka or milk, coins, small sculptures. When passing an *ovoo*, travelers stop, walk around it three times clockwise, and make their prayer. It is a gesture of spiritual continuity: that the physical journey is also a cosmic journey.

Ovoo are not simple monuments. They are portals. There, prayers ascend. There, spirits descend. During rituals, the shaman might summon ancestors to "sit" upon the *ovoo* and listen to the clan. Some families have their own *ovoo*. Others share tribal *ovoo*. In major festivals, *ovoo* are adorned with new cloths, cleaned of debris, and reactivated with chants and juniper smoke. Some *ovoo* are so ancient their layers tell the tribe's history – each stone, a generation; each tie, a promise made to the Sky.

Water sources are also deeply respected. Springs and rivers are not mere resources – they are beings. Each spring has its spirit, its *iye*. Offending it – by urinating there, throwing trash, diverting water without permission – is considered a very serious fault. Shamans sometimes go to these waters to receive visions. And before major decisions, many dive into or drink from these springs, asking for clarity and blessing. There are specific springs for fertility, others for healing, others for poetic inspiration. In some valleys, there are stones that "weep" water – and these earth tears are seen as the Mother's tears.

Forests also harbor sacred sites. Areas where sounds seem muffled, where light penetrates differently.

There live ancient spirits, guardians of plant and animal life. Some trees are considered dwellings of these beings – especially the oldest, gnarled, solitary ones. Around them, cloth strips are tied, food left, or chants sung. Cutting one of these trees without permission is inviting misfortune upon oneself. In many cases, a shaman must intercede to "calm" the offended spirit.

There are also grottos and caves, associated with the underworld. They are avoided not out of fear, but respect. Entering a cave is traversing the earth's womb. Before entering, it's customary to light a flame, offer tobacco or honey, and ask permission. Some of these caves are sites of shamanic initiation. There, the apprentice spends days fasting, listening to what stones have to say. When emerging, reborn, they are no longer the same.

Space is also sacred in nomadic tents and homes. The yurt's center – where the fire is – is the house's spiritual heart. Around it organizes not only furniture, but the very flow of life. It is there prayers are made, elders listened to, the dead honored. Therefore, newborns are presented to the fire, and the dying placed near it. The fire witnesses everything.

With modernity and urbanization, many of these sacred sites were threatened, forgotten, or adulterated. But the revival of Tengriism brought a counter-movement: rediscovering, restoring, reconsecrating these places. Pilgrimages have been organized to ancient sanctuaries. Spiritual groups rebuild destroyed *ovoo*. Scholars identify mountains mentioned in legends and return them to the people. A spiritual geography is being rebuilt, stone by stone.

Even those living far from the steppes can create a sacred site. A corner in the yard where something is planted with intention. A stone brought from a mountain resonating something deep. An improvised altar with symbols linking to the Sky. The sacred site is less about where it is on the map, and more about what is felt there. It is where the heart silences, the soul listens, time changes.

Sacred sites, therefore, are not merely inheritances of the ancestral landscape – they are living territories continuing to pulse in the spiritual memory of those still knowing how to listen to the earth. When visited with reverence, these places offer not only visions and blessings: they remind humans of their role within the world's order. Each rebuilt *ovoo*, respected spring, offered stone is a reattached link in the subtle chain between visible and invisible. Sacredness resides not in the physical space itself, but in how humans position themselves before it: with humility, listening, reciprocity.

This relationship between place and spirit transforms the experience of geography into something profoundly ethical. Being in a sacred site is also being observed by it. The traveler, pilgrim, or even common resident becomes part of the rite, part of the living landscape. Recognizing that the mountain, river, or tree also has memory and presence dissolves the logic of possession and establishes that of coexistence. In the Tengriist world, walking the earth is walking among consciousnesses. And therefore, each step must be taken with respect. The territory is not inert – it is interlocutor.

It is this restored listening that allows sacred sites to continue existing, even outside their homeland. A silent balcony can become a point of reconnection. A carefully brought stone can serve as an anchor for the spirit. In times of dispersion and inner exile, creating and recognizing sacred sites is an act of healing. A gesture of remembrance. Because where true intention exists, where silent attention and living presence are found, there too dwells the sacred. And once found, this place is never forgotten – it remains, waiting, like an old friend who never stopped calling.

Chapter 17
Buddhist Syncretism

The blue sky covering Mongolia has seen more than passing clouds and moving herds. It saw the silent fusion of religious worlds, the meeting of ancient shamans with new lamas, steppe spirits sitting side by side with Himalayan bodhisattvas. This encounter was not a collision, but an intertwining. The syncretism between Tengriism and Lamaist Buddhism did not dissolve one faith into the other – it created a spiritual tapestry where shamanic and Buddhist threads interwove, each retaining its color, but composing a common fabric.

When Buddhism arrived in Mongolia in the 16th century, brought by Tibetan influence and reinforced by internal pacification policies, it found fertile ground, but one already inhabited by a powerful ancestral religion. Mongols were no strangers to the idea of a Supreme Sky, invisible spirits, sacred pilgrimages. Tengriism was ingrained not only in ritual practices but in the worldview, stories told around the fire, khans' decisions. Therefore, Buddhism imposed itself not by force, but dialogue, often mediated by hybrid figures – shamans who were also monks, lamas respecting *ovoo*.

This process gave rise to the so-called "Yellow Shamanism," a religious practice mixing Buddhist precepts with traditional shamanic rites. The color yellow, symbol of Tibetan Buddhism, tinged many aspects of Mongolian spiritual life, but without erasing Tengri's celestial blue. Many ceremonies began including both mantra recitation and shamanic drum use. Nature spirits continued being invoked, but their names sometimes transformed into Buddhist epithets. Offerings to ancestors persisted, but were accompanied by incense and images of Buddhist deities.

This coexistence was facilitated by a very particular Mongol perception: for many practitioners, there was no conflict between believing in Tengri and revering Buddha. One was the Eternal Sky, omnipresent cosmic principle; the other, an enlightened master teaching the path to liberation. The Sky did not exclude Buddha. On the contrary, made space for him. Thus, popular spirituality shaped itself around the idea that there are multiple paths under the same sky – and that all enlightened beings, whether shamans or buddhas, ultimately serve the cosmic harmony desired by Tengri.

The figure of Genghis Khan was a central point of this syncretism. Already venerated as ancestor and spiritual hero by Tengriists, he began being reinterpreted within Buddhist tradition as a kind of *dharmapala* – a protector of the dharma, a force that, though warrior-like, was aligned with cosmic order. There are records of temples where Genghis is depicted alongside Buddhist deities, receiving offerings as an elevated ancestral spirit. In popular narratives, he is seen as someone who acted with the Eternal Sky's blessing, but also with the wisdom of a warrior bodhisattva.

This mixture took shape not only in rituals but also in sacred art. Thangkas painted in Tibetan style began including shamanic elements – world trees, totemic animals, sacred mountains. Some representations of Buddhist deities were reinterpreted shamanically: Green Tara, for example, was associated with the goddess Umay; Padmasambhava, tantric master, was seen as an "enlightened shaman" dominating spirits. This reinterpretation was not imposed by doctrines but sprang from the people's lived experience, the need to make sense of the new without abandoning the old.

In the ritual field, syncretism produced fascinating formulas. An *ovoo* could be consecrated with Buddhist prayers but receive shamanic offerings – milk, stones, colored cloths. Lamas recited sutras at events beginning with invocations to ancestors. On some occasions, lamas themselves consulted shamans for spiritual diagnoses or healings. There was a kind of mutual recognition: the shaman mediated with spirits, the lama with texts and precepts. Both dealt with the invisible, each in their own way.

In Mongolia's interior, far from urban centers, many families maintained a dual spirituality. Visited Buddhist monasteries for blessings, but still called shamans for healing rites or house protection. For generations, Buddhism and Tengriism coexisted on domestic altars: a Buddha statue beside a shamanic drum; prayer beads next to a talisman made of bone or stone. No inconsistency was seen in this – continuity was seen.

There were, naturally, tensions. Some lamas sought to erase shamanic practices, branding them superstition. There were attempts at faith "purification," especially during periods of greater institutionalization of Buddhism. But Tengriism survived in the margins, in daily gestures, in prayers murmured softly. And in times of political repression – like during the communist regime – it was often shamanism that kept popular spirituality alive, hidden in songs, legends, practices disguised as family tradition.

Today, with the revival of spiritual traditions in Mongolia and other regions of Central Asia, this syncretism is viewed with new eyes. For many young Mongols, practicing Tengriism does not mean rejecting Buddhism – it means recovering a forgotten part of their identity. In modern festivals, it's common to see ceremonies combining elements of both traditions. There are even inter-spiritual initiatives seeking to revive "Yellow Shamanism" with contemporary awareness, uniting ancestral practices with modern values of respect for spiritual diversity.

In the academic field, scholars like Baatarjav, Nyam-Osor, and others have researched the interface between Tengriism and Buddhism, showing how syncretism shaped not only rituals but worldviews, forms of government, and daily ethics. It was discovered that many traditional moral teachings – like respect for elders, compassion for animals, the search for balance –

are sustained by this religious encounter and not by the imposition of a single doctrine.

This syncretism is, therefore, more than religious fusion. It is an adaptive response, a form of cultural survival. It proves that a living tradition does not break before the new – it bends, molds, incorporates, transforms. Tengriism, with its spiritual flexibility, allowed Buddhism to flourish without annihilating ancestral roots. And Buddhism, with its philosophical depth, offered Tengriism a new language to express itself.

The symbiotic survival of Tengriism and Buddhism in Mongolia also reveals a broader truth about human spirituality: faith is not a fixed entity, but a living organism breathing to the rhythm of cultural transformations. In the Mongolian scenario, this malleable spirituality generated not only religious practices, but ways of being in the world. Children growing up hearing stories about ancestral spirits also learned about the merits of Buddhist compassion. Healing rituals were not limited to the body but reached the soul, through symbols crossing boundaries between sky and teaching, drum and sutra, smoke and enlightenment.

Furthermore, Mongolian syncretism broke with the binary view of the sacred as exclusive or hierarchical. Instead of creating a new orthodoxy, it allowed multiple coexistences, where the shamanic drum's force echoed without contradicting the monasteries' meditative silence. This generated a religiosity not closing itself in dogmas, but opening in layers, adapting to life's seasons and spirit's demands. Even those leaning more towards philosophical Buddhism often unconsciously carried archaic Tengriist gestures – like reverence for mountains, rituals with milk, respect for nature's cycle. Each gesture was a bridge between worlds.

What remains, more than any doctrine, is the Mongol people's ability to preserve meaning in history's folds. Between steppe winds and monastery silence, between the drum's fire and prayer wheels' gleam, a spirituality woven of continuity and transformation was created. This is syncretism's invisible legacy: not the fusion erasing margins, but the intertwining respecting them. An ancient thread still pulsing under new forms, reminding that a people's soul, like their land's blue sky, is vast enough to welcome many lights.

Chapter 18
Ancestral Resistance

The passing clouds of the steppe carry more than wind and dust: they bear ancestral memories, echoes of prayers whispered against oblivion. Tengriism, persecuted, veiled by other religions, and erased from official books, did not disappear. It hid. It abandoned centers and retreated into the deep valleys of the nomadic soul. It crossed centuries in silence, veiled by songs shamans taught grandchildren before dying, preserved in simple gestures like throwing milk to the sky or lighting the home fire with reverence. This was the resistance of those refusing to forget who they were, even if they could no longer say their name aloud.

In northern Mongolia, where winds whistle among hills and cattle roam free under the deep blue, emerged what scholars call "Black Shamanism." Unlike "Yellow Shamanism," permeated by Buddhist influence, the black guarded what was earlier, what was pure. Its practitioners, usually hunters, herders, and families distant from cities, kept ancient rites alive in secret. It was knowledge passed mouth-to-mouth, without documents, monks, temples. Knowledge was in bones, dreams, dawn chants. And thus, for centuries, these groups sustained steppe spirituality against civilizing tides trying to drown it.

But Mongolia was not the only stage for this resistance. In Siberia, the brutality of the Tsarist empire and, later, the systematic terror of the Soviet era made Tengriism a clandestine practice. Peoples like the Yakuts, Buryats, Tuvans, and others hid their faith under Christian symbols, adopting saints secretly corresponding to ancient gods or spirits. When missionaries asked who that protected spirit was, they answered with a name acceptable to the Orthodox Church. But in their hearts, they knew it was Ayı, or the forest spirit, or the soul of the grandfather who turned into a bear after death. This spiritual camouflage did not erase the cult – merely dressed it in new clothes.

During the darkest years of the Soviet regime, in the 1930s, Tengriism was harshly persecuted. Shamans were captured, tortured, sent to labor camps. Their drums, considered instruments of superstition and subversion, were burned in public squares. Survivors learned silence. But not all fell completely silent. In wooden cabins, on frozen riverbanks, people still danced around fires, still told the story of the World Tree, still taught boys that the sky is not just sky, but an invisible father seeing everything.

Communist repression was violent, but not omnipotent. Old women preserved prayers in lullabies. Young men listened to stars' whispers while riding alone across plains. Even when rituals could no longer be performed openly, the spirit of resistance remained in language, symbols, tales never ceasing to be told. This is

Tengriism's nature: it entrenches itself, needs no altars or doctrines. It is in the earth's bones and the people's breath.

In the empire's south, among Kazakhs and Kyrgyz, Islam expanded, bringing the book, mosque, law. But it did not take away ancient rituals. They merely transformed. Animal sacrifice remained, but gained the name of Islamic offering. Tribal sanctuaries continued being visited, now under the name "mazar." Ancestral lineage was venerated no longer as part of Tengriism, but as a respectable cultural tradition. The bridge was Sufism – a mystical Islam, open to ecstasy, direct vision, poetic reverence for the divine. There, Tengri and Allah could coexist for a time. Men like Ahmad Yasawi brought this fusion to light, using nomadic terms and steppe imagery to speak of God. The children of the blue sky began pronouncing the Prophet's name, but still raised eyes to the same silent vastness where they had always sought guidance.

In the Kyrgyz epic "Manas," the intertwining is noticeable. Allah is mentioned, true. But heroes still converse with spirits, still receive visions, still live according to animal and dream omens. Tengri's presence is not erased – merely renamed. In the subtext, the old sky remains.

This shows resistance was not always combative, sometimes strategic. Tengriism knew how to survive like groundwater, deviating from obstacles, infiltrating under dominant religions' foundations, awaiting the moment to resurface. And that moment came. In the late 20th century, after the USSR's collapse, what was hidden began emerging with unexpected force. Survivors – descendants of murdered shamans, grandchildren of elders still secretly throwing milk to the sky – began organizing. Gathered in squares, founded spiritual centers, rebuilt destroyed *ovoo*. Shame gave way to pride. What for decades was reason for persecution became an identity banner.

In Ulaanbaatar, Mongolia's capital, shamans began serving people publicly. In Tuva, throat singing echoed again in festivals. In Yakutia, solstice rituals gained status as official cultural celebrations.

But it wasn't a simple return. Long repression left deep marks. Many rituals were partially forgotten, needing reconstruction based on fragments, legends, anthropological observations. Authenticity was questioned: what is tradition and what is reconstruction? For some, it matters little. What's important is the ancestral spirit being alive, even in new forms. For others, distinguishing ancient from modern invention is necessary. Amidst this debate, contemporary Tengriism forms – hybrid, mutable, but still bearing an ancient flame that refused extinction.

This flame burns not only on steppes. Today, it ignites hearts in urban centers, among young people who never knew nomadism but feel an inner call not coming from books or churches. A call from the open sky, the diffuse memory that once their ancestors rode free under immense stars, answering only to the Eternal Sky. It is this feeling – of freedom, cosmic belonging, spiritual dignity – moving them to resume rituals, sing ancient names, ask grandmothers what was never said.

This ancestral resistance, therefore, is not just reaction to past oppression. It is also a proposal for the future. It shows there are ways of living not bending to time. That faith needs no temples or dogmas – just a drum, a respectfully piled stone, a breath released to the wind with sincerity. Tengriism survived because its essence is in the invisible, unsaid, transmitted by gestures and silences. Survived because it is in the blood of those who never stopped listening to the sky.

In recent years, this spiritual rediscovery has manifested not only as return to the sacred, but also veiled critique of cultural homogenization imposed by modernity. In an era of rapid consumption and canned spirituality, Tengriism's resurgence offers a radically rooted alternative: living attuned to earth cycles, honoring the dead with silence and fire, accepting the invisible as part of the real. For many young people, rediscovering Tengri's spirit is also refusing the logic of large centralized religions, betting on a spirituality lived in the body, landscape, collective memory of a people who never completely knelt.

This reconstructed spirituality—sometimes fragmented, sometimes reinvented—seeks not just restoring the past, but creating new forms of belonging. Among steppe and mountain peoples, networks of spiritual connection emerge mixing oral traditions with modern technologies, ancestral calls with current languages. Resistance is now also done through documentaries, intercultural festivals, contemporary art, and music resonating ancient drums on urban stages.

This movement is not attempt to return to what was, but continuation. Reinvented continuity, unafraid of contradiction, but faithful to the ancient pulse still echoing in northern winds. And perhaps this is the greatest victory of those who resisted silently: seeing their legacy flourish, not as museum piece, but living force. Tengriism needed not win wars nor write sacred scriptures. It sufficed to remain—in secret, in gestures, in home ashes. And now, with eyes turned skyward, a new generation hears again the invisible's call, not as nostalgia, but direction. Because wherever there is respect for earth, listening to ancestors, and reverence for sky, there Tengri's spirit will never have died.

Chapter 19
Tengri and Islam

Between the open skies of the steppes and the minarets of mosques rising on the horizon, there was a time when two spiritual worlds met. On one side, ancient Tengriism – worship of the Eternal Sky, nature spirits, ancestors. On the other, Islam – with its single God, written revelations, defined rituals. This convergence happened not by abrupt imposition nor forced mass conversion, but by a subtle, continuous process of syncretism, where concepts of the blue sky and the invisible God began mirroring each other.

The spiritual heart of Turkic peoples, for centuries, was anchored in the idea of Tengri. The Sky, with its silent vastness and invisible justice, was more than a deity – it was the cosmos' ordering principle, the father seeing all. When the first Muslim missionaries reached steppe regions between the 8th and 10th centuries, they found tribes already believing in a single celestial God, albeit with polytheistic practices associated with earth spirits and ancestors. This facilitated a religious dialogue that, instead of destroying ancient beliefs, began assimilating them under new names.

Sufis, especially, were fundamental in this encounter. Men like Ahmad Yasawi, 12th-century poet, mystic, preacher, spoke of Allah in the nomads' language. In his verses, Allah is simultaneously Creator and Sky, source of light and destiny. Yasawi used images of mountains, rivers, eagles – deeply Tengriist symbols – to explain God's oneness. This adaptation was not artifice: it was the natural expression of a man recognizing in his own heart both Islam's wisdom and ancestral reverence for sky and earth.

Not coincidentally, many Islamic terms were molded after native words. Instead of "Allah," Turks began using "Tanrı" – a direct translation of Tengri, still resonating today in languages of Kazakhstan, Turkmenistan, Turkey. Expressions like "Tanrı Türkü Korusun" ("May God protect the Turks") are common in nationalist contexts, but also carry the echo of an older spiritual past. In daily prayers, even practicing Muslims might refer to God with names of Tengriist roots, thus maintaining an invisible bridge between Islam and their pre-Islamic heritage.

During the Middle Ages, Muslim chroniclers and travelers noted with perplexity, sometimes disapproval, how Turkic peoples combined Islamic devotion with ancestral customs. Mahmud al-Kashgari, for example, wrote that Turks bowed before mountains, trees, other natural elements – practices he considered heretical, but showing Tengriist animism's persistence even among converts. For Turks, there wasn't necessarily contradiction: Sky, Mountain, Wind – all were expressions of the same God, just manifested differently.

In subsequent centuries, Islam established itself as the dominant religion among Central Asian Turkic peoples, but never completely erased worship of the Eternal Sky. Kazakh, Kyrgyz, Karakalpak tribes and others maintained their *ovoo*, sacred stone mounds where they made offerings, even after mosques were built. Ritual animal sacrifices, common on the steppe, continued being performed in Allah's name, but ritual sites and forms still recalled the Tengriist past.

In festivals like Nauryz – the steppe New Year, celebrated at the spring equinox – elements not derived from the Quran, but from ancient solar and fertility cults, are commonly found. During these days, entire families visit sacred sites, wash in rivers, make offerings to earth and ancestors, ask the sky for blessings. Many consider these actions just part of "national culture," but their root is clearly spiritual, born from times when the sky was the only temple.

Islam's language, with references to heaven as God's dwelling, facilitated symbolic fusion. Just as the Quran speaks of God's Throne above seven celestial layers, Tengriism describes seven heavens where elevated spirits reside. Just as Islam values fasting, prayer, purification, Tengriism teaches moderation, reverence, ritual cleansing – not as commandments, but ways to align human with cosmos. The correspondence between practices and values allowed a more fluid coexistence than seen in other rival religions.

Still, tensions existed. With the advance of orthodox Islamic schools and organized religious authorities, especially from the 16th century, many Tengriist elements began being seen as superstition or heresy. Ulemas condemned consulting shamans, venerating *ovoo*, belief in multiple souls, divination practice – central pillars of Tengriism. Despite this, popular faith continued practicing such customs, albeit discreetly, away from clerics' eyes.

In modern times, Tengriism's resurgence provoked diverse reactions among Muslims. In some countries, like Kazakhstan and Kyrgyzstan, relatively peaceful coexistence exists. It's common for the same person to attend a Tengriist ceremony one weekend and go to mosque on Friday. For many, these aren't opposing religions, but complementary spiritual languages: one speaks to the sky from inside out, the other from outside in. One is collective, public, written; the other intimate, silent, experience-based.

On the political plane, nationalist leaders used Tengriism as an identity symbol, contrasting it with Islam as a foreign religion from the Middle East. Figures like Ziya Gökalp in Turkey and other Pan-Turkist ideologues tried resurrecting the ancient faith as a mark of cultural purity, striving to strengthen ethnic pride and unity among Turkic peoples. This instrumentalization generated tensions with more conservative Islamic movements, viewing Tengriism as disguised paganism.

But among common people, reality is more complex and serene. The old blue sky is still greeted in folk songs. Mothers still teach children to respect nature, as "Tengri sees everything." Herders still make milk offerings to the soil before heading to pastures. And, simultaneously, recite Quranic surahs and ask Allah's blessing. This syncretic coexistence is the true legacy of the fusion between Tengriism and Islam – not complete fusion, but continuous dialogue, reflection of the Turkic way of seeing the world as whole, not irreconcilable duality.

Looking at this long coexistence between Tengri and Allah, one realizes the essential was never belief uniformity, but a people's ability to integrate visions without betraying roots. The spiritual Turk lives not the tension of theological dilemma – lives the fluidity of a worldview accepting the sacred can speak multiple languages. Between prostration before the mihrab and the gesture of throwing milk on the ground, there is no conflict, there is continuity. The Eternal Sky and the single God become faces of the same search: finding in the invisible the order governing life, honoring what came before and what is yet to come.

This possible harmony challenges rigid doctrines trying to control faith like fencing the wind. The steppe people know the sky cannot be parceled. Therefore, Turkic spirituality resists simplification and remains vast as the horizon. Even in contemporary urban societies, this way of believing reflects in how time is marked, earth treated, the dead remembered. It is a religion of margins, fitting neither temples nor orthodoxies, but living – whole – in daily gestures and silent pauses amidst nature. Because, ultimately, what remains is not belief dispute, but the echo of a people who never stopped listening to the sky. Words may change, rites adapt, but the impulse to lift eyes seeking meaning remains the same. Islam may have renamed faith, but Tengri's spirit taught the people to hear silence between words. And it is in this space – between Quran and steppe wind, mosque and *ovoo* – that still pulses the soul of a people who never saw contradiction in venerating both sky and the God speaking of it.

Chapter 20
Tengri and Christianity

When steppe winds met Western crosses, a new chapter began in the interaction between Tengriism and major world religions. Between Central Asian desert sands and European church bells, the paths of the Eternal Sky and the Christian God intertwined surprisingly. The Mongol Empire, with its vastness and diversity, became the stage for this unlikely rapprochement. More than a meeting of beliefs, it was an exercise in mutual interpretation, where categories of faith, power, identity reorganized under Tengri's aegis.

In the 13th and 14th centuries, as Mongol legions expanded from Manchuria to Hungary, their leaders demonstrated unprecedented religious flexibility. This tolerance was not just pragmatic but reflected an inclusive cosmogonic view. For a traditional Mongol, all religions spoke of different aspects of the same supreme Sky. Names changed, rituals varied, but the eternal principle – the Blue Sky, omniscient and just – was universal. This conviction allowed figures like Genghis Khan, Kublai Khan, Hulagu Khan to dialogue with Christians, Muslims, Buddhists without abdicating authority conferred by Tengri.

Diplomatic relations with Christian kingdoms, especially France, Crusader states, Byzantine Empire, reveal much about this religious interface. In letters sent by Hulagu Khan to King Louis IX and other Christian monarchs, the Eternal Sky is repeatedly mentioned as the source of Mongol power. Genghis Khan himself was described as Tengri's chosen one, the "lord of nations" instituted by divine will. In these missives, the Christian God is not denied – is incorporated. Jesus Christ is called "Misica Tengrin," i.e., Messiah of Tengri, an incarnation of the living Sky. This symbolic appropriation aimed not at syncretism in the modern sense, but reflected Mongol spiritual logic. For them, Christ was a sacred spirit sent by the same Sky guiding steppe shamans. Like the buddha or Muslim prophet, he was recognized as bearer of a spark of the Eternal. This view allowed Christianity not to be seen as heresy, but one of many legitimate manifestations of celestial will. Faith was not a doctrine competition, but a network of paths leading to the same absolute firmament.

Several Turkic and Mongol tribes adopted forms of Christianity, mainly the Nestorian branch, spread throughout the East since early centuries AD. Among Keraits, Naimans, other clans, Christian missionaries found fertile ground. But Christianity there didn't develop as in the West. It was tinged with local colors: Christian symbols combined with celestial images, rites mixed with traditional sacrifices, saints revered as glorified ancestors. The cross, in many cases, appeared alongside wolf amulets or the World Tree.

The figure of Doquz Khatun, Hulagu Khan's wife and devout Christian, is emblematic. She sponsored churches, protected clergy, influenced important political decisions in the Persian Ilkhanate. However, even she – like all Mongol nobles – recognized the Eternal Sky's supremacy. Spiritual loyalty to Tengriism did not exclude practicing another faith. The Bible's God could be venerated, as long as not contradicting Tengri's primacy, the principle sustaining imperial power's legitimacy and cosmic order.

This view allowed symbolic fusion: the Christian God was translated as "Tengri," and Christ seen as one of this Sky's envoys. Mongol terminology made no rigid distinction between supreme deity and physical sky – both expressed mystery. This semantic plasticity facilitated Christianity's incorporation into the nomadic ethos. Instead of monumental temples, open-air sanctuaries; instead of formal liturgies, chants honoring Sky and ancestors; and instead of systematized theology, experiential spirituality.

Mongols never saw Christianity as threat. Unlike Islam, sometimes trying to impose itself in dominated regions, Nestorian Christianity adapted easily to local cultures. Missionaries learned native languages, respected customs, didn't demand exclusive worship. This allowed peaceful coexistence between beliefs. There were baptized Mongols still making offerings to *ovoo*, consulting shamans, celebrating ancestral rituals. In the steppe mentality, everything was part of the same spiritual fabric: sky, cross, eagle, shamanic drum.

On the symbolic plane, Christianity provided images and narratives enriching the Mongol imaginary. Jesus' crucifixion story, for example, was reinterpreted in light of ritual sacrifice: the Messiah suffering for humanity recalled the white horse offered to the Sky in times of crisis. Scripture angels appeared as winged celestial beings, similar to spiritual entities shamans claimed encountering in visionary journeys. The Holy Spirit, as divine wind, was associated with Tengri's manifestations in storms and breezes speaking to nomads' hearts.

In the Mongol Empire's westernmost regions, like Crimea and Caucasus, some Mongol and Turkic communities were absorbed by Orthodox faith. However, even when churches replaced sacrificial fields, the sky continued being greeted. Sun, moon, star worship persisted discreetly, camouflaged in liturgical calendars and popular habits. For centuries, families clapped towards the sky on cold winter mornings, murmuring prayers not found in psalms, but in the steppe soul's millennial winds.

The Christianization of Tengriist peoples was not total conversion, but symbolic superposition. Tengri was never banished – merely acquired new names. In many regions, he survived as the deep layer of collective spiritual consciousness, even when crosses were erected and bells began ringing. In times of crisis, ancients were still consulted, sacred fires lit, and above all, the Blue Sky's approval sought.

Today, in countries like Kazakhstan, Kyrgyzstan, parts of Mongolia, Christian communities live alongside practitioners of revitalized Tengriism. Symbols intersect: crosses hang beside blue ribbons on sacred trees; churches are built near *ovoo*; Christians still call God Tengri without hesitation. This is not heresy – it is memory. A memory not erased, but transformed, resisting centuries' passage like the sky remaining, even when clouds change shape.

This intertwining between Tengri and the Christian God produced not doctrinal synthesis, but a kind of spiritual echo – mutual recognition between two distinct ways of accessing the sacred. Ultimately, both pointed to a common origin: the desire to understand what exists above and beyond, what orders the world and confers meaning to existence. Steppe nomads saw in Christianity not a threat to ancestral faith, but a possible extension, a new story that could be welcomed without renouncing the Blue Sky. Christ bleeding for humanity and the drum pulsating under the sky were both distinct answers to the same millennial question.

This spiritual openness, so typical of steppe cultures, also challenged models of exclusive, centralized faith. Unlike the institutional rigidity marking certain Christian expressions, Tengriism taught the divine could be multiple in appearance, though one in essence. Therefore, even when crosses were planted on pastoral lands, they didn't nullify *ovoo* – merely added to the spiritual landscape. The steppe became a space of cross-resonance: where Christ's name echoed among drums, and Tengri's breath still made sacred trees' leaves vibrate.

What remained, beyond church ruins and ancient shamans' bones, was this invisible thread connecting sky and cross, ancestral spirit and foreign faith. A silent heritage, made more of gestures than dogmas, reverence than imposition. In the eyes of those still lifting heads to greet the dawn sky, there is no contradiction – there is remembrance. Because, regardless of the name given the divine, what moves the human heart is always the same: the search for meaning before the infinite. And in this infinite, Tengri still dwells, not as forgotten past, but living presence under all forms of faith.

Chapter 21
Secular Modernity

The dawn of the 20th century raised a new firmament over the peoples of the steppes. However, this time it was not Tengri ruling the laws of the sky, but an ideology promising progress, equality, and science as the only legitimate deities. Secular modernity – especially in the form of Soviet communism and Asian authoritarian regimes – made the spiritual past a threat to order, a superstition to be eradicated, a shadow hindering the arrival of "rational light." Against this new orthodoxy, Tengriism did not wage frontal war. It retreated. Silenced. Hid in the folds of popular memory, waiting.

In the Mongolian People's Republic, established in 1924 with direct Moscow support, a systematic policy of eliminating spiritual traditions began. Although the main target was Lamaist Buddhism – with hundreds of monasteries destroyed and monks exterminated – shamanism and Tengriism were also targeted. Shamans considered "charlatans" or "reactionary elements" were arrested, confined to psychiatric hospitals, or summarily executed. Sacred rituals came to be seen as "feudal remnants" and traditional symbols as enemies of socialist progress.

In the USSR, the scenario was even harsher. Peoples like the Yakuts, Buryats, Tuvans, Khakassians – all heirs of regional forms of Tengriism – were subjected to aggressive campaigns of cultural assimilation. Schools taught scientific atheism, shamanic drums were confiscated and burned, ancestral festivals replaced by secular, depoliticized celebrations. Russification of names, imposition of the Cyrillic alphabet, centralization of community life around state institutions further diluted traditional spiritual identity. Entire families began hiding their rites, making offerings in secret, burying sacred objects in the ground, feigning conformity to survive.

Communism was not the only vector of secular modernity. The rise of nation-states in formerly nomadic territories brought developmentalist ideologies viewing indigenous spiritual practices as obstacles to progress. In Kazakhstan and Kyrgyzstan, for example, forced sedentarization of nomads, combined with Soviet-model schooling, produced an intergenerational rupture. Young people raised in cities learned about Marx, Lenin, Gagarin, but no longer knew the names of mountain spirits their grandparents still feared.

This transition was profound and, in many ways, irreversible. The linear, technical worldview of the modern world – based on resource exploitation, instrumental rationality, science supremacy – left no room for a universe animated by spirits. The very notion of "sacred" was ridiculed or reduced to the private, folkloric sphere. Rituals, when tolerated, were transformed into tourist attractions or cultural events devoid of religious meaning. The drum became accessory. The *ovoo* became photo backdrop. The sky, once source of spiritual authority, became just atmosphere.

Accelerated urbanization played a crucial role. In expanding metropolises, herders' children became civil servants, engineers, teachers, merchants. Yurts gave way to concrete blocks, the sacred home fire replaced by piped gas. Nature, which in Tengriism was living temple, became distant landscape – seen from a bus window, commented on in documentaries, but rarely experienced as source of mystical connection. Spiritual nomadism lost ground to consumption sedentarism.

This forced secularization generated a kind of internal spiritual exile. Many people, though having assimilated modern values, carried a vague sense of loss, displacement. The sky was still there, blue and immense, but no longer spoke. The earth remained fertile, but its voice was no longer heard. Dreams ceased being ancestral messages and began being interpreted by psychologists. The collective meaning of the world – sustained by generations of rites and myths – was fragmented by a modernity teaching each should find their own path, disconnected from lineage and landscape.

In the final years of the USSR, this absence began weighing. In the 1980s, with economic crisis and widespread disillusionment with communism, the first signs emerged of a desire for reconnection. Even among the most secularized, there was a diffuse nostalgia for something "authentic," "ours," "ancestral." Old songs began being sung again at family parties. Grandmothers started telling forgotten myths to grandchildren. In rural areas, domestic rituals – like pouring milk on the ground or greeting the rising sun – persisted discreetly, almost like automatic gestures, but charged with deep meanings.

This spiritual residue was not erased. It remained like ember under ash, ready to rekindle when the wind of freedom blew again. With the Soviet Union's collapse in 1991, this wind finally came. And with it, an urgent search for identity, meaning, roots. But before that, for over seventy years, Tengriism survived in silence. Its language became subterranean. Its signs encoded in folklore, gestures, popular expressions. It was an invisible spirituality, but not extinct – like the sky itself, continuing above clouds, even when unseen.

Secular modernity erased not only beliefs but redesigned internal maps of belonging and meaning. In cities shaped by concrete and ideology, bonds previously uniting human to cosmos were replaced by promises of measurable progress. However, this new world, though efficient, lacked rootedness. Tengriism, with its reverence for the invisible and ancestral rhythm, began inhabiting the collective unconscious, like a dull echo insisting on resonating in moments of silence. The absence of rite and myth produced a void neither scientific manuals nor political slogans could completely fill.

The spiritual exile imposed by modernity produced not just cultural rupture, but existential shock. Not just loss of belief, but of a way of being in the world, interpreting nature's signs and one's own feelings. Even those not consciously recognizing this grief carried the restlessness of a nameless memory, a longing unexplainable in present terms. Thus, Tengriism, far from being just religious tradition, began representing subterranean resistance—a web of meanings that, though frayed, remained present in the folds of daily time.

With the end of the regime seeking to silence steppe gods, this web could finally begin reconstruction. The sky never ceased being there, and when eyes turned upward again, found something familiar. Not total restoration, but restart. What had been hidden by fear began being rediscovered with desire. The future, then, began being dreamed not as denial of the past, but reconnection with what survived even under history's ashes.

Chapter 22
Current Revivalism

When the shackles of ideological repression finally broke with the Soviet Union's collapse, an ancient song began echoing again in Central Asia's mountains and plains. It was not just folkloric revival. It was the rebirth of an ancestral spiritual voice that had been silenced, but never forgotten. Tengriism, which for decades remained dormant in the shadows of collective memory, emerged from ashes like a beacon of rediscovered identity. Instead of disappearing under modernity's weight, it resurfaced with new strength, now embraced by intellectuals, artists, rural communities, and urban youth seeking belonging.

In the 1990s and early 2000s, newly independent Central Asian republics underwent intense national reconstruction. Amidst the urgent need to create distinct symbols – separate from both Soviet heritage and external religious influences – many leaders and cultural movements turned to the nomadic past seeking authentic foundations. It was in this context Tengriism found fertile ground to flourish. No longer seen as archaic superstition, but as the spiritual cradle of Turco-Mongol peoples, a link uniting culture, territory, cosmos.

Kazakhstan became one epicenter of this movement. There, figures like Nursultan Nazarbayev, first president of the independent country, extolled Tengriist heritage as a pillar of Kazakh identity. Although the state officially maintained religious neutrality, Tengriist symbols began being exalted in public ceremonies and official documents. The flag's turquoise blue color, solar patterns, references to "Blue Sky" gained new meaning. Intellectuals and historians began reinterpreting ancient heroes as defenders of ancestral faith, proposing a spiritual reading of national past.

In this context emerged Dastan Sarygulov, one of Tengriist revivalism's most prominent names. In 2005, he founded the group Tengir Ordo – literally "Order of Tengri" – aiming to promote ethics based on traditional values and reconnect the Kyrgyz people with their spiritual root. For Sarygulov, Tengriism wasn't just religion: it was a worldview, a life philosophy deeply ecological and humanistic. His initiative inspired other organizations, and public events began incorporating rites and symbols previously viewed with suspicion.

In Russia, revitalization also gained momentum, especially in autonomous republics where indigenous peoples still maintained connection with ancient spiritual practices. Tuva, Yakutia (Sakha), Buryatia, Khakassia became poles for revaluing Tengriist shamanism. In Tuva, for example, the "Federation of Siberian Shamans" formed, gathering practitioners who kept tradition alive even during Soviet times. These shamans began operating publicly, offering healing sessions, divination, spiritual counseling in urban centers, while performing collective rituals on sacred dates, like the summer solstice.

Yakutia stands out particularly. There, the "Aiyy Faith" – a local branch of Tengriism – gained status as a legitimate spiritual movement, with partial popular support and state tolerance. The Yhyakh festival, for example, transformed into a major public celebration where thousands participate in outdoor rituals, sing ancestral chants, pay homage to celestial deities and Mother Earth. This event, though now also attracting tourists, retains its spiritual core and is seen by many as a way to reconnect with ancestors.

Mongolia, Genghis Khan's birthplace and land where sky seems to touch earth on every horizon, also saw shamanism reborn vigorously. With legalization of traditional spiritual practices, dozens of urban shaman groups emerged, many serving both rural areas and large cities like Ulaanbaatar. Centers like the Golomt Center became references in training new practitioners and conducting public rituals. Urban youth, often alienated from traditional teachings, began attending these ceremonies seeking something missing in conventional religions or Westernized modernity's values.

But the revival didn't occur only among direct descendants of ancient Tengriist peoples. Tengriism's ecological, non-dogmatic spirituality began attracting interest from people of other cultures. Spiritual travelers, scholars, sympathizers of animism saw in this tradition a profound response to contemporary crises – especially environmental crisis and sense of spiritual alienation.

Open ceremonies began receiving foreign participants, and translations of myths and shamanic teachings gained circulation in European languages.

This international interest, however, brought tensions and challenges. On one hand, fears of tradition commodification – self-declared shamans offering spiritual experiences to tourists at high prices, simplified ceremonies pleasing Western taste, appropriation of sacred symbols in contexts outside their worldview. On the other, voices within the movement itself defend openness, intercultural dialogue, adaptation to the modern world. Argue Tengriism was always flexible, adapting to different realities without losing essence.

This tension between authenticity and innovation is also visible in media representations of revivalism. Epic films about nomadic heroes, music videos with shamanic aesthetics, documentaries on ancestral spiritual practices – all helped popularize the theme, but also risk transforming Tengriism into empty aesthetics, disconnected from ritual and symbolic depth. Therefore, many practitioners advocate serious training, learning from experienced masters, respect for spiritual lineage.

Despite challenges, revivalism's impact is undeniable. In recent censuses, about 8% of Yakuts declared following "Aiyy Faith," and in public ceremonies in Kyrgyzstan and Kazakhstan hundreds gather to offer milk, vodka, chants to the Sky. Youth groups create online communities to study Tengriist mythology, exchange experiences, organize meetings. Books, podcasts, documentaries, even video games inspired by nomadic cosmology begin appearing, offering a bridge between past and future.

Modern Tengriism, therefore, is not mere reenactment of the past. It is a living tradition, in constant transformation, seeking to respond to present needs with ancient tools. It demands not blind adherence, but proposes a path of listening, reconnection with Earth, Sky, ancestors. A path tread silently, with a handful of milk offered to the wind, or in collective celebrations before the sacred fire.

The contemporary revival of Tengriism reveals not just a rescue movement, but an active process of symbolic reinvention, where the past is shaped by present urgencies. In societies suffering erasure of identity matrices, returning to ancestral spiritual practices serves both as resistance and reintegration. This process isn't homogeneous, nor free of contradictions: assumes distinct forms in each region, according to political contexts, local interests, tensions between tradition and modernity. However, what unites these manifestations is the search for rooted spirituality, capable of offering meaning and belonging in an accelerated, fragmented, often dehumanized world.

At the same time, Tengriism's language – made of cosmic symbols, nature-linked ritual practices, community values – seems to dialogue uniquely with global issues. Its circular time view, respect for natural forces, ethics based on harmony with environment offer a radical alternative to utilitarian logics now prevailing. This resonance extrapolates ethnic or geographical borders: becomes contact point between distinct worlds, where a young steppe nomad and an urban European environmentalist might find the same spiritual vibration, albeit via different paths. This doesn't eliminate superficiality risk, but points towards possibility of shared spiritual ecology.

Ultimately, Tengriist revivalism acts as mirror and compass. Mirror, reflecting the lack of meaning felt by many facing dissolution of old faith and culture structures. Compass, pointing to possible reconnection paths – with Earth cycles, community bonds, sacred silence between Sky and wind. And perhaps, more than seeking ready answers, it is this reverent listening to the invisible that is the true legacy of a tradition which, though ancient, knows how to be reborn with the present's breath.

Chapter 23
Spiritual Search

The drum's flames resonate not only in Central Asian mountains but within a yearning growing silently in the contemporary human heart. The spiritual search pervading the early 21st century reveals more than mere curiosity about forgotten traditions: it is an ancient hunger, an existential thirst that large urban centers and technology's promises failed to quench. In this globalized scenario, where consumption replaced rituals and speed erased silence, the return to ancestral practices like Tengriism points to a deeper movement – the return to the essential, the connecting.

Tengriism's rediscovery occurs in a time marked by paradoxes. Never so much information available, yet sense of belonging seems to vanish. Never so many visible organized religions, yet growing numbers declare themselves "spiritual but not religious." It's in this void of everyday transcendence that many, especially descendants of Turco-Mongol peoples, begin looking back, to winds whispering prayers under their ancestors' blue sky, to piled stones guarding simple offerings to Mother Earth.

Tengriism offers no dogma nor demands submission. Conversely, its strength lies in lived experience, direct contact with the sacred. Unlike many institutionalized traditions presenting clergy, scriptures, rigid orthodoxies, Tengriism invites perception of the invisible through nature and ancestry. This openness makes it attractive not only to peoples descending from it, but also spiritual seekers worldwide, feeling something was lost on the modern path and seeking to rediscover a more organic, living spirituality.

Among urban youth in Kazakhstan, Mongolia, Kyrgyzstan, many report a feeling of returning "spiritual home" upon contacting Tengriist myths, rituals, cosmology. It transcends ethnic pride or cultural rescue – though these are present. What moves these people is reconnection with something seemingly silenced: awareness that earth is alive, sky hears, ancestors walk with us. A spirituality based not on promises of afterlife, but deep communion with the sacred present.

At the same time, this search crosses geographical borders. In the West, interest grows in animist, shamanic, ecocentric traditions. Tengriism appears on this horizon as an authentic, ancestral, little-explored alternative. Its worldview imposes no salvation, but proposes balance. Condemns not, but guides. Through worship of Tengri, Mother Earth, nature spirits, ancestors, practitioners find not only protection, but a way of life where every gesture – from lighting fire to picking an herb – is charged with meaning.

These elements explain why, in recent decades, Tengriist ceremonies have attracted participants of diverse origins, not just nomadic or rural, but also scientists, therapists, artists, environmentalists. At events like the Yhyakh Festival in Yakutia, or spiritual gatherings at Lake Issyk-Kul, one sees not only traditional shamans conducting rituals, but also university students, civil servants, foreigners with closed eyes in reverence, learning to greet the four winds. There is no catechism. There is connection. And that is what so many seek.

Another aspect of this spiritual search is the sense of absence installed by modern secularization. Post-industrial societies broke traditional bonds, leaving many individuals adrift between productivity, entertainment, competition. Even among the religiously affiliated, there's a lack of concrete spiritual experience – sky ceased being sacred, earth became resource. In this context, Tengriism's rediscovery functions as anchor, reminder there's another way to inhabit the world: not as owners, but children.

At the heart of this search also lies the desire for reconciliation with one's own ancestors. For many young people who grew up distant from their cultures' oral and spiritual traditions, Tengriism is a bridge between modernity and memory. Learning the names of deities, spirits, rites is recovering a seemingly extinct spiritual language. And this learning occurs not just in books or conferences, but in the body – participating in a fire ritual, touching a sacred drum, hearing the mountain's silence and understanding a spirit dwells there.

It's also notable how Tengriism resonates with sustainability and ecological awareness values emerging in the contemporary world. In times of climate crisis,

Tengriism proposes not just attitude change, but perception change: earth is not resource deposit, but living mother; water is not market commodity, but blood of sacred rivers. This view doesn't romanticize nature, but recognizes it as a living spiritual system, with which one must negotiate, respect, thank. Therefore, many see in Tengriism a profoundly ecological spiritual path – a sacred response to the environmental urgency we face.

The return to traditional spirituality doesn't occur without conflicts. Resistances exist within and outside communities. Among organized religious, some see Tengriism as superstition or idolatry. Among secularists, some ridicule it as outdated folklore. But those practicing it seek not to convince. For them, what matters is lived experience: offering milk to the sky at dawn, listening to wind omens, honoring ancestors around the fire. Simple gestures, but re-enchanting life. And in this silent reunion with the everyday sacred lies the answer to our times' spiritual search.

There's yet another layer: the personal search for healing. Many turn to Tengriism in moments of crisis – emotional, physical, existential. Find in rituals, shamans, symbolic practices a way to deal with suffering modern medicine and psychology often fail to reach. Hearing a drum resonating like the world's heartbeat, or being enveloped by herb smoke in a purification rite, the individual feels part of something larger. This experience, in itself, is therapeutic – not because promising miracles, but restoring sense of belonging and continuity.

The depth of this spiritual search cannot be measured by statistics or public declarations. Often it happens silently, in withdrawal. An elder lighting fire as his grandfather did; a young woman learning her lineage's forgotten chants; a family building a small *ovoo* in the garden, among flowers and stones. Discreet gestures, but repeated by thousands, constitute a spiritual current growing day by day.

The silent nature of these gestures reveals the movement's deepest essence: not adhering to a system, but remembering something already inhabiting each person's ancestral memory. The return to Tengriism, in this sense, happens not as conversion, but awakening. The lit fire, whispered chant, respect for natural cycles – all compose an intimate liturgy, where the sacred isn't imposed, but emergent. This spirituality needs no grand temples, finds shelter in sky's vastness, ancestors' invisible presence, winds' attentive listening. It invites full presence, reunion with a time not running, but pulsing.

Therefore, even when invisible to formal religious structures, the contemporary spiritual search takes shape in daily life. Amidst sleepless cities, some close eyes to hear a distant mountain's call; amidst constant network noise, some choose silence to light incense and converse with their dead. These practices, often solitary, become threads of a great spiritual tapestry woven without fanfare. Tengriism, in this context, is not isolated phenomenon, but part of broader movement reconnecting with spirituality not dividing world into profane and sacred, but understanding it as single living, interdependent body.

This awareness, though in state of rescue, returns to humans a symbolic place in cosmos – not master, but participant. Perceiving oneself again as part of whole, the individual rediscovers inner axis, direction not depending on absolute answers, but sensitive, attentive walking. Thus, spiritual search ends not in sudden revelation, but unfolds like ancient trail rediscovered underfoot. And it is in this silent step-by-step, this humble return to essential, that the sometimes exhausted contemporary soul finds rest.

Chapter 24
Siberian Shamanism

Siberia's vastness, with dense taigas, silent tundras, winding rivers, has sheltered millennia-old peoples relating to the world deeply spiritually. In this setting where winter lingers and nature imposes severe rhythms, flourished a myriad of shamanic traditions that, though diverse in cultural expressions, share a common core with Turco-Mongol Tengriism. Siberian shamanism isn't uniform religious system, but living tapestry of experiences, myths, practices demonstrating how humans, even in extreme conditions, built bridge of constant dialogue with invisible.

Among Yakuts (or Sakha), Buryats, Evenks, Tuvans, Khakass, other Siberian peoples, the shaman – whether called *oyuun*, *böö*, or *kam* – is central figure. He not only heals and advises but sustains link between worlds. Roots of this shamanism delve into pre-literate, pre-state times, preserving archaic spiritual structures dialoguing directly with earth cycles, constellations, animal rhythms. The tripartite cosmology dividing universe into three spheres – upper, middle, lower world – is trait shared with Tengriism, suggesting common wisdom background between steppe and Siberian forest peoples.

Belief in spiritual beings inhabiting rivers, trees, mountains, animals is omnipresent among Siberian peoples. Yakuts, for example, speak of *Aiyy*, set of superior celestial spirits resembling Tengri figure. There's also worship of Yer Su (earth and water), present in various Turkic languages, reaffirming divine dual pattern manifested in sky and earth. Ancestral spirits are also venerated, not as past memories, but active presences accompanying, protecting the living. In many Siberian homes, small altars with ancestor photos, ritual objects indicate this continuity between visible and invisible world.

Among Evenks and Buryats, shamanic drums are considered not just instruments, but sacred entities endowed with soul. When played, open portals allowing shaman to travel between worlds. Drum isn't just sound vehicle, but mystical mount – spiritual horse or reindeer transporting shaman's spirit on journey. This image resonates with symbolism found in Tengriism, where horse is also mediator between man and Sky. Drum view as living being, with beats and breath, reveals world perception where objects also possess life, spiritual agency.

In many Siberian rituals, shaman invokes auxiliary spirits – *ongon* or *yehin* – assuming forms of animals, nature elements, even specific ancestors. These entities aren't merely symbolic: are felt, perceived, incorporated. Ritual possession practice is common, shaman temporarily yielding body for spirit to bring messages or perform healings. Words spoken in this state considered oracular, deserving attention, reverence.

This direct contact with supernatural isn't restricted to shaman: many community members, especially sensitive ones, report visionary dreams, premonitions, spontaneous spiritual experiences, reinforcing Siberian religiosity's participatory, experiential character.

Comparing these practices with Tengriism, we perceive that though deity names vary, spiritual functions remain. Siberian shaman, like Mongol *böö* or Turkic *kam*, is mediator, healer, counselor, visionary. Knows hidden paths linking three worlds, knows how to restore balance when broken – whether by illness, conflict, natural disasters. This function isn't learned from books, but transmitted by lineage, initiations, near-death or spiritual illness experiences preparing chosen one's body and spirit for mission.

Important to stress that despite structural similarities, each ethnicity developed unique characteristics. Among Khakass, for example, local mythology includes god Kurbustu, warrior celestial figure, while Yakuts develop more hierarchical pantheon, with entities like Ürüng Aar Toion (White Lord Above), occupying role analogous to Tengri. Presence of mother goddesses is also notable – female spirits linked to fertility, water, child protection. Evenki revere entities called Xoni, associated with forest, while Buryats maintain cults to mountain spirits, like Khan Khokhii. This diversity enriches Siberian spiritual mosaic, reveals shamanism's plasticity as living system, adaptable to environments, community needs.

During Soviet rule, these traditions were violently repressed. Shamans arrested, executed, forced into silence. Their drums destroyed, songs forbidden. Yet, survived. Hidden in remote houses, mixed with "folkloric" rituals, disguised under Christian symbolism, ancestral knowledges continued being transmitted from grandmother to grandson, master to apprentice. This spiritual underground wasn't extinguished – just dormant, awaiting moment to bloom again. And that moment came.

With Soviet Union's fall, Siberia saw emergence of new shaman generation, spiritual associations, festivals openly celebrating native religiosity. Revival is visible, and with it, dialogue with classic Tengriism intensified. In inter-shamanic meetings held in places like Ulan-Ude, Kyzyl, Yakutsk, spiritual leaders from diverse ethnicities share knowledge, myths, healing techniques. There's mutual recognition: though each invokes gods and spirits by own names, all refer to same sky, same invisible world pulsating behind visible. Terms like "neo-Tengriism Siberian" emerge designating this convergence movement, though many prefer simply "ancestral way." For these practitioners, concern isn't theological definition, but living experience of reconnection with spiritual and natural world.

Similarity between Siberian shamanism and Tengriism shouldn't be confused with absolute identity. Multiplicity is part of what gives these traditions strength. However, undeniable there's common symbolic field: tripartite worldview, heaven and earth veneration, ancestor worship, belief in nature spirits, shaman's role as axis between dimensions. This common field legitimizes idea of "Eurasian spiritual belt" extending from Hungary to North Pacific forests, encompassing peoples as distant as Uralic Hungarians and Japanese Ainu. In all, same invisible thread links human, spirit, cosmos.

Nowadays, Siberian shamanism has crossed cultural borders. Therapists, scholars, spiritual seekers worldwide approach these traditions, not as exotic spectators, but learners. Siberian drum workshops, juniper purification ceremonies, sacred mountain pilgrimages—all became part of new global spiritual map where indigenous wisdom rediscovered as antidote to modernity's ills. Some warn of undue appropriation risks; others see diffusion as opportunity for intercultural dialogue, survival for threatened knowledges.

Siberian shamanism's openness to contemporary world doesn't mean dilution, but reveals ancestral force knowing how to adapt without losing depth. As outsiders approach these knowledges, change perceived not just in diffusion, but listening: some come not to translate, but learn humbly. This listening is fundamental, as shamanism transmitted not just by words, but presence, silence, rhythm, inner vision. What's offered, then, isn't manual or promise, but invitation to shed certainties, walk barefoot on ancestors' living earth.

Still, for Siberian peoples themselves, rediscovering spiritual roots isn't just individual practice: is political, cultural act. Reviving ancient chants, restoring collective rituals, transmitting myths to new generations is also form of resistance against global homogenization. It's in reintegrating these elements many rediscover history's dignity, identity's strength. Shamanism, in this context, ceases being just spiritual tradition, becomes path of collective healing, where reconnection with invisible translates into belonging, memory, community reconstruction.

Amidst Siberia's icy vastness, the drum continues sounding. And its echo resonates far beyond forests and steppes sheltering it for centuries. Crosses borders, touches seekers' hearts, reactivates seemingly forgotten spiritual sensitivity. No matter language used invoking spirits, nor name given sky: gesture is same, call is same. And as long as there are those singing to mountain, offering milk to fire, listening to wind's whisper as sacred word, Siberian shamanism will remain alive — not just as heritage, but path.

Chapter 25
Indigenous Traditions

When the world spirit whispers through ancestral trees, blows across deserts, rises in eternal mountains, it speaks many languages. And among voices listening, responding to this call, are those of indigenous peoples scattered across continents – communities that, though separated by oceans, converge in perceiving Earth is alive, Sky is conscious being, human is just part of vast cosmic network. Just as Tengriism flourished on Eurasian steppes and taigas, similar spiritual traditions emerged in Americas' heart, African savannas, Andean plateaus, Pacific islands, Southeast Asian forests. Spirit of sacred natural is universal, its reverberation in indigenous myths and rituals evidences human soul deeply attuned to life's mystery.

Among North American natives, Great Spirit figure is central. Known as Wakan Tanka among Lakota, Gitche Manitou among Algonquians, Tirawa by Pawnee, he is supreme, invisible presence permeating all. This conception isn't distant from Tengri, Eternal Sky: both are non-anthropomorphic, omnipresent beings, manifesting in nature forces, guiding human destinies. North American plains Indians, for example, revered open sky, eagles in flight, winds crossing prairies – elements recognized as sacred, like in Tengriism. Sun Dance, one of these cultures' most important rites, symbolized direct connection with Sky Spirit, evoking strength, healing, guidance.

Further south, Amazonian forest peoples built spirituality deeply intertwined with exuberant biodiversity surrounding them. Yanomami *pajés*, Kayapó shamans, Guarani spiritual leaders – all recognize in animals, plants, rivers entities endowed with will, wisdom. A vine can contain goddess spirit; jaguar might be reincarnated ancestor; river can speak, in dream, to healer. Use of entheogens, like ayahuasca, common facilitating dialogue with these hidden worlds. Not search for individualistic "enlightenment," but collective communion, aimed at village and surrounding nature balance. Deep respect for forest spirits echoes Tengriist veneration for *iye* – spiritual guardians of each natural entity.

In Africa, pantheon of deities and spirits in traditional religions reveals notable parallelism with Asian steppes' animist worldview. Among Yoruba, for example, exists Olodumare, supreme being creating all, and orishas, natural and spiritual manifestations of his will. Shango is thunder, Oshun river, Iansã wind – natural forces become consciousnesses. Although sub-Saharan Africa possesses more hierarchical religious structure in certain cultures, base remains recognition of soul present in nature, communication between living and ancestors. Idea shaman, priest, or babalawo can mediate between worlds, traveling in trance, consulting spirits, guiding living, directly recalls role of Tengriist and Siberian shamans.

In Pacific archipelagos, Maori peoples of New Zealand, Samoans, Tongans, Hawaiians develop traditions where ocean, volcanoes, winds considered alive. Notion of *mana* – sacred vital force permeating all – approaches idea of "kut" or "nefes" in Tengriism: vital breath animating humans, animals, even objects. Respect for ancestors fundamental in these island cultures. Genealogies sung, ancient names revered, sacred sites maintained as portals to spiritual world. Sea isn't just food source, but path between worlds. Ocean crossing becomes, then, not just physical, but mystical – many rituals involve requests for protection to sky and sea before any journey.

On Andean highlands, Quechuas and Aymaras worship Pachamama – Mother Earth – with fervor, devotion. This figure almost identical to Tengriism's Etugen: both represent fertile soil, nurturing mountain, silent goddess sustaining life. Pachamama cult not restricted to symbolic offerings, manifests in seasonal rituals, community festivals, fasts, constant thanksgivings. Just as Turkic nomads threw milk skyward in reverence, Andeans pour *chicha* (corn beverage) on earth before drinking, offering goddess her share. Reciprocity is base of relationship with divine – idea present in all indigenous traditions and also Tengriism: if you respect spirits, they protect you; if ignore or disrespect, fall silent or turn against you.

Three worlds structure also common to diverse indigenous cosmologies. Guarani, for example, speak of

Nhanderu – celestial father dwelling in upper world – and underworld inhabited by negative or chaotic forces. Forest shamans, like Shipibo-Conibo of Peru, describe journeys climbing "cosmic trees" or diving into "rivers of light" linking different reality planes. World Tree – so central in Tengriist view – appears in other forms: sacred palm, magic vine, colossal trunk supporting sky. These images, though culturally distinct, point to common human mind archetypes: vertical connection between worlds, spiritual mediator traveling between them, need to maintain balance between planes.

Important to note that despite similarities, each culture expresses truths with unique symbols, shaped by environment, history. Mongol shaman's drum might equate Amazonian *pajé's* maraca; horse as spirit-guide might be exchanged for hummingbird or jaguar. Symbolic languages vary, but spiritual structure remains remarkably convergent. This led many scholars, like Mircea Eliade, Michael Harner, to suggest existence of primordial shamanic matrix – spirituality form rooted in prehistoric human condition, survived in multiple globe points via indigenous traditions.

This universality also opens paths for intercultural dialogue between living traditions. In international ancestral spirituality meetings – like those held by UN in indigenous rights forums or global ecospiritual networks – representatives from different peoples share chants, rituals, visions. Buryat shaman might dialogue with Hopi leader; Ainu woman might share symbols with Maori priestess. In these exchanges, expression often heard: "Earth unites us." And, in many cases,

Tengriist practices recognized as spiritual sisters of global indigenous beliefs – different in form, equal in foundation: reverence for life, respect for ancestors, communication with invisible.

Even in diasporas and urban contexts, indigenous peoples' descendants seek keeping these connections alive. In São Paulo, New York, Paris, small communities hold full moon ceremonies, gratitude rituals, traditional dances. Similarly, Mongol, Buryat, Tuvan emigrants recreate symbolic *ovoo* in large cities' parks, maintaining spiritual contact with roots. Many young mestizos or with hybrid cultural identities find in these practices way to integrate diverse belongings – whether indigenous, modern, Western, spiritual. Tengriism and other native traditions offer, then, not just cultural heritage, but path of healing, identity reintegration.

This multiplicity of spiritual expressions, spread across world's indigenous cultures, reveals not just symbolic diversity, but same essential gesture: listening to Earth, dialoguing with invisible. Each people, with myths, rites, chants, translated this gesture according to territory's pulse – whether sound of maracas, drums, flutes, or reverent silence before mountain. It's in this active listening ancestral thread linking humans to cosmos preserved, thread not breaking with time, but renewing with each ritual gesture, simple offering, story told by fireside. Therefore, though each tradition has own language, particular cosmology, mutually recognize each other as variations of same wisdom: that sacred is here, on ground we tread, in wind blowing, in eyes of those who came before.

Contemplating this vast spiritual cloth, becomes evident indigenous traditions aren't stuck in past, but continue offering answers to present. In times marked by ecological crises, existential disorientation, community bond rupture, teachings appear as keys for reconciliation with life. Doesn't mean idealizing or appropriating them, but learning from reciprocity ethic, spirituality incorporated into daily life, way of knowing world through affection, listening. Each encounter with these traditions can be, therefore, opportunity to realign with own humanity – one feeling, dreaming, celebrating existence mysteries around fire, under open sky.

Thus, when descendants of these cultures, even in urban, fragmented contexts, seek reviving rituals, aren't just rescuing roots, but activating futures. Drum playing on concrete terrace carries same call as one resonating on free plains; offering made with herbs gathered in urban garden possesses same intention as one made in forest heart. Ancestral spirit demands not geographical purity, but gesture truth. And as long as there are those singing to Moon, dreaming with animals, seeing in thunder ancient god's voice, indigenous traditions will continue reminding we aren't separated from world – are part of it, deeply intertwined in its song.

Chapter 26
Ecological Vision

At the core of Tengriist spirituality pulses a perception of nature not as passive backdrop to human existence, but divine protagonist of a grand sacred narrative. Earth is alive, Sky is conscious, rivers breathe, mountains dream. For Tengri's devotee, each natural world element carries spirit deserving reverence, dialogue, reciprocity. This conception isn't late romantic idealization; intertwined in daily practices of tradition born from nomadism, flourished in Eurasian steppe womb. Tengriism, therefore, offers more than religion – offers ecological ethic rooted in millennial experience of harmonious coexistence with natural world.

Relationship between human and nature in Tengriism isn't subjugation, but co-participation. Human isn't Earth's master, but its child. This truth echoes in tradition's central cosmogonic myth: human being is fruit of union between Sky (Tengri) and Earth (Etugen). Earth, in this sense, isn't resource exploited to exhaustion, but nurturing mother sustaining life with generosity, power. Metaphor isn't decorative – defines behaviors, shapes decisions, structures entire civilization on balance principles. Caring for earth, waters, air, fire is caring for oneself, as all share same spiritual lineage.

Nomadism of Turkic and Mongol peoples favored worldview where nature is travel companion, not enemy tamed. Nomads need renewed pasture, clean springs, fertile soil – know none exists without respect for things' natural rhythm. Herd must rest land; river must run unobstructed; trees cut with permission, parsimony. These peoples, by necessity and wisdom, developed deep observance of natural cycles. Seasons, star movements, animal behaviors – all were signs, sacred language. And disrespecting this language seen as sin against cosmic balance.

This ecological ethic manifests concretely in traditional rituals. Before cutting tree, family head might ask forest spirit's permission, pour milk or vodka on ground as offering, pronounce words of respect. Sacrificing animal, moment of silence where living being's soul thanked for meat donation. Nothing done mechanically or indifferently – every action has spiritual consequence. River pollution, for example, seen not just environmental crime, but offense to those waters' guardian spirit. And offending spirit can bring illness, bad luck, droughts. Thus, Tengriism's ecological codes are also survival codes.

Fire is sacred. Water is sacred. Wind is sacred. Earth is sacred. Not because abstract symbols, but manifestations of real, perceptible, present forces. Shaman, tradition's central figure, not only evokes these elements during ceremonies – dialogues with them. Fire in tent center isn't just heat source, but mouth through which worlds communicate. Wind entering yurt skylight carries gods' messages. Incense smoke takes human desires to heavens. Each nature element is link between visible and invisible.

In contemporary context of global ecological devastation, this ancestral vision resurfaces as urgent, powerful alternative. Modern world, guided by unlimited consumption, exploitation logic, faces climate collapse, species extinction, natural resource depletion. In this scenario, Tengriism proposes value inversion: abandon idea nature serves man, embrace idea man must serve, protect nature. Not by abstract moral obligation, but practical wisdom – for environment destruction is self-destruction.

Some contemporary Tengriist communities, aware of this, engage in ecological actions inspired by ancient principles. Shaman groups in Siberia perform periodic ceremonies to "feed" mountains, rivers, lakes – bringing offerings, singing purification chants. In Kazakhstan regions, young ecological activists organize forest, spring cleaning drives, followed by thanksgiving rituals to local spirits. Rural Mongolian schools incorporate Tengriist teachings into curriculum, encouraging students see animals, stones, clouds as parts of spiritual community.

This ecological spirituality isn't limited to activism. Redefines success, progress notion. Where modern world sees wealth in accumulation terms, Tengriism sees wealth in balance terms. Prosperous tribe isn't one accumulating most, but respecting earth cycles most, living peacefully with spirits. Wisdom measured not by technical mastery, but ability listen nature, interpret signs. Ideal leader isn't most powerful, but most attuned to Sky and Earth will.

Tengriist aesthetics reflect this spiritual ecology. Blue, green colors predominate in flags, attire, ritual objects. Blue like infinite sky, green like living plains. Traditional music made with instruments imitating natural sounds: wind whistle, horse trot, stream murmur. Songs celebrate not human achievements, but creation beauty, place spirits, totemic animals. Shaman's drum pulses like earth heart; throat singing resonates like cave echo. All creates aesthetic not alienating man from world – but re-inscribing him as creature among creatures.

Not coincidentally, Tengriism attracted attention from environmental movements, ecospiritualists, contemporary seekers looking for more authentic, harmonious way being in world. Many recognize in steppe spirituality forgotten but vital wisdom. Idea spirituality isn't separate from ecology – soul care and planet care are one thing – finds echo in new generations uneasy with modern civilization's course. Tengriism, in this sense, isn't just ethnic relic – is future proposal.

Though practices might seem distant from current urban life, principles sustaining Tengriism universal, adaptable. Voluntary simplicity, conscious consumption, cycle respect, earth gratitude, invisible listening – all can be practiced anywhere. Urban garden can be consecrated with Sky prayers. Glass of water drunk with awareness of spirit inhabiting substance. Park walk can become reconnection rite. Important isn't external form, but inner feeling reverence, reciprocity.

This ethic of care, listening contrasts sharply with culture of speed, productivity, nature objectification. Tengriism proposes different rhythm – closer to seasons, lunar cycles, cloud movement rhythm. Proposes also different economy – based on sufficient, communal, sacred. Not about regressing to past, but extracting seeds of new vision from it. Vision where progress means not domination, but maturation; technology serves not exploit, but preserve; spirituality reduces not to formal rituals, but expands as lifestyle.

This reconnection between spirituality and ecology, proposed by Tengriism, gains even more relevance when we realize present environmental crisis isn't just resource crisis, but imagination crisis. How we see world shapes how we treat it. And if for centuries view prevailed separating human from rest of creation, now urgent cultivate perception reintegrating us into whole. Tengriism, presenting Earth as mother, Sky as father, offers not just poetic metaphors, but symbolic map inhabit planet with humility, gratitude. Wisdom not competing with scientific knowledge, but complementing it, reminding world care is also spiritual act.

As we face global warming, water scarcity, biodiversity collapse, soil impoverishment, becomes clear technical solutions alone insufficient. New (or ancient) paradigm needed – way thinking, feeling recognizing life sacredness in all forms. Tengriism proposes no ready formulas, but values rooted in listening, reciprocity, presence. Teaches each daily gesture – planting, harvesting, thanking, asking permission – can be ritual, each being – stone, animal, wind, star – has something say, if learn listen. Sensitive learning transforming relationship with planet, ourselves.

Ultimately, Tengriism's ecological vision invites spirituality of belonging. Not seeking transcendence outside world, but diving deeply into it, recognizing interdependence uniting us to all existing. Understanding requires not all become nomads or shamans, but cultivate tenderer, more attentive gaze towards life around. In times climate urgency, existential uprooting, this return to essential – fire in center, observing sky, nurturing earth – can be starting point for new path. Path not separating sacred from mundane, nor human from nature, but recognizing them as single continuous breath of life.

Chapter 27
Modern Practices

Amidst the spiritual re-enchantment of the 21st century, many seek practices that transcend mere empty ritual and reconnect with deep experiences of meaning. Tengriism, with its non-dogmatic essence and intimate connection to nature, presents itself as a viable and potent path. However, the question facing those who wish to follow this path today is: how to live Tengriism far from the vast steppes, the ancestral rituals in their full form, and daily interaction with traditional shamans? The answer lies in the adaptability of this ancient tradition, which, even without sacred texts or a central ecclesiastical structure, maintains an internal coherence that allows its authentic recreation in new contexts.

The modern practitioner of Tengriism, often living in cities, far from tribal territories and sacred mountains, reinvents their forms of devotion based on the same principles that guided the ancient nomads: respect, reciprocity, and direct connection with the sacred. There's no need for grand temples or complex liturgies. Simplicity is a virtue.

One of the most common practices among contemporary devotees is the daily gesture of offering a little milk, tea, or vodka to the sky, the ground, or the fire. At dawn, tossing a few drops to the wind while uttering words of gratitude to Tengri constitutes a minimal yet profound rite. It is a recognition of the miracle of being alive under the Eternal Sky. This practice, derived from the traditional offerings of Mongol and Turkic herders, can be performed even from an apartment window or in an urban backyard. The setting doesn't matter—what counts is the intention and feeling. It's an act of reaffirming the sacred bond between the human and the elements. For many, this daily gesture becomes a kind of active meditation, a spiritual realignment with the forces sustaining life. Feeling the wind on one's face and perceiving Tengri's presence in it, observing a tree and greeting the spirit inhabiting it, hearing a bird's song as if it were a message from the invisible—all this makes up the daily life of the modern Tengriist.

Another very present form in the contemporary revival of Tengriism is the construction of small domestic shrines inspired by traditional *ovoos*. Piling some stones in the garden, tying ribbons of blue and white silk (sacred colors), and dedicating this space as a symbolic dwelling for the spirits of earth and sky creates a focal point for devotion. These structures, however small, function as spiritual anchors. There one can pray, meditate, make offerings, or simply be silent. Some families gather weekly around the domestic *ovoo*, rekindling ancestral ties, sharing food, and invoking blessings for the household members. The *ovoo* thus becomes not just an altar, but a link of belonging and continuity.

The use of the shamanic drum has also been reclaimed in many urban contexts. Study and practice groups formed by descendants of Turkic and Mongol peoples, as well as those interested in nature spirituality, have dedicated themselves to learning the rhythmic beat that induces altered states of consciousness. The drum is not seen as a musical instrument, but as a vehicle for crossing. It leads the practitioner into sacred space, into contact with the protective animal spirit or with the forces of the invisible world. Through the pulsating sound, the body resonates with the cosmos. Those who learn to play the drum ritually report intense experiences of emotional healing, spiritual insights, and a deep sense of reconnection with something larger than themselves.

Although many modern practices are adapted to daily urban life, there is also a growing movement of symbolic return to nature. In various regions of Central Asia and Siberia, practitioners organize pilgrimages to sacred sites like lakes, mountains, or ancient forests. On these occasions, open ceremonies are held with collective participation. Offerings are made to the four winds, traditional chants are sung, and communion with local spirits is celebrated. These experiences not only strengthen spiritual identity but also create support networks among practitioners sharing the same values. In more remote areas of Mongolia, such gatherings resemble ancient nomadic festivities, with tents set up, food shared, and dancing around the fire.

Then there are the healing rituals, which continue to be performed, albeit with modern nuances. Urban shamans, trained by traditional masters or family lineages, attend to patients with emotional, spiritual, or psychosomatic problems. In many cases, these rituals include smudging with herbs, use of drums, and prayers in ancestral languages. People suffering from anxiety, depression, or a sense of emptiness find in these encounters an alternative to Western models of treatment. For shamans, illness is often an expression of an imbalance between the individual and the forces of nature. Restoring this balance is the goal. The shaman doesn't heal alone—he invokes and cooperates with spirits, acting as a channel and mediator.

It's important to note that modern Tengriism doesn't claim to be an exclusive religion. Many of its practitioners simultaneously identify with other traditions. It's not uncommon to find someone who declares themselves Muslim or Buddhist but maintains Tengriist practices at home. This occurs because Tengriism, in its essence, requires no conversion, nor promises of dogmatic loyalty. It is an open, inclusive spiritual practice, centered on the direct experience of the sacred in nature and ancestry. Therefore, many consider it more a "worldview" or "way of life" than a formal religion. This fluidity makes it particularly attractive in a world marked by cultural hybridity and the search for authenticity.

The internet plays a decisive role in this contemporary re-signification. Forums, social media groups, and video channels connect practitioners scattered around the world, allowing exchanges of experiences, learning, and strengthening of a common spiritual identity. There are videos teaching how to make domestic *ovoos*, chant traditional songs, use specific herbs in smudging. Books and introductory manuals to Tengriism adapted to modern reality, with accessible language and practical focus, are also emerging. This democratization of spiritual knowledge helps the tradition stay alive and evolve without losing its essence.

Youth have also embraced Tengriism creatively. Cultural festivals with Tengriist inspiration, blending modern music with spiritual themes, have become popular in cities of Mongolia, Kazakhstan, and Kyrgyzstan. At these events, bands play traditional instruments with contemporary arrangements, poets recite verses about the Blue Sky, and visual artists exhibit works depicting ancestral deities and mythical scenes. At the same time, educational movements seek to include Tengriism as part of the historical and cultural curriculum of public schools, promoting ethnic pride and respect for religious diversity.

Even outside Central Asia, Westerners touched by the natural philosophy of Tengriism incorporate elements of the tradition into their lives. In European countries and the Americas, small groups celebrate the solstice with rituals inspired by *ovoos*; practitioners of animist spiritualities see Tengriism as a distant sibling, sharing a common origin. This international openness doesn't dilute the tradition—rather, it broadens its reach and reiterates its universal value. After all, reverence for the sky, the earth, and the spirits of nature is not the monopoly of one people—it's a deep human longing.

The contemporary expansion of Tengriism demonstrates that tradition survives not just through the repetition of ancient formulas, but through its capacity to be felt and reinvented in diverse contexts. Spirituality, in this sense, reveals itself less as a set of prescriptions and more as a living field of relationships and experiences. The modern practitioner doesn't seek to copy ancient rituals exactly, but to evoke the same spirit of presence, humility, and listening that sustained the bond with the Eternal Sky. In a world saturated with distractions, Tengriism offers a silent way of reunion with what is essential—not through escape from the modern world, but through the re-signification of every gesture, every gust of wind, as a portal to the sacred.

By integrating into multiple cultural realities, Tengriism reaffirms its essence not as a closed system, but as a spiritual language capable of dialoguing with different ways of being and believing. This malleability makes it particularly valuable in times marked by identity fragmentation and the search for meaning. What unites practitioners is not uniformity of dogma, but a common perception: that the universe is alive, that everything existing is interconnected, and that humans, to live fully, must honor this web of relationships. Thus, whether through a drum beaten in the heart of the metropolis, a blue ribbon tied to a dry branch, or a word whispered to the sky before breakfast, the spirit of Tengriism remains intact—pulsing with the same force as the steppes of yore.

In this reunion between the ancestral and the contemporary, Tengriism resurfaces not as a relic of a lost time, but as a living and relevant presence. It offers a serene response to modern tumult, reminding us that the sacred is not distant, but inhabits the everyday—one only needs to recognize it. By restoring sacredness to the world, the contemporary practitioner of Tengriism not only preserves a tradition but also transforms themselves and the spaces they occupy, creating bridges between past and future, sky and earth, the visible and the invisible.

Chapter 28
Values and Ethics

In the invisible tapestry sustaining Tengriism, values and ethical principles do not present themselves as rigid commandments or written codes imposed from the outside in. On the contrary, they emerge from the organic spiritual experience of nomadic peoples, as a natural expression of a worldview where the universe is understood as a living, interconnected organism. Right and wrong are not defined by external impositions but intuited from careful observation of nature, human relationships, and the consequences of one's own actions. The Eternal Sky, witness to all that occurs beneath its blue mantle, is the mirror against which each person measures their righteousness.

To live according to Tengri means, above all, to live in balance. Balance here is not understood as a simple absence of conflict, but as a dynamic harmony between the complementary forces of life: sky and earth, man and woman, action and contemplation, community and individual. All excess is viewed with suspicion because it disrupts the flow of vital energy sustaining the world. Avarice, greed, cruelty, disrespect for elders or nature are considered forms of transgression against the cosmic order. Generosity, courage, loyalty, respect, and gratitude are virtues that keep the fabric of the universe cohesive and healthy.

Hospitality, for example, was not a luxury or a choice among the peoples of the steppe—it was a sacred obligation. The vast, inhospitable expanse demanded solidarity: denying food or shelter to a traveler could mean condemning them to death and, by extension, attracting the disapproval of spirits. Welcoming guests warmly, sharing the herd's milk, offering the tent's fire were expected gestures from any honorable person. This ethic of sharing reflected the understanding that nothing belongs to us completely—everything is a temporary gift granted by Tengri and must circulate. Wealth, when accumulated without community purpose, was seen as a sickness of the soul. True prestige lay in generosity, not possession.

Another fundamental value is honor—a concept far exceeding social reputation. Honoring one's word, maintaining loyalty to blood ties and allies, acting righteously even when no one is watching: all this makes up the image of the integral human being in Tengri's eyes. In many historical accounts, oaths made to the Sky were considered inviolable. Breaking them could attract curses not only upon the individual but upon their entire lineage. The awareness that one's soul is shaped by actions and intentions, and that ancestors observe the behavior of the living, generated continuous ethical responsibility.

Good and evil were not absolute concepts but were always related to the impact of actions on the overall balance. Reverence for elders and ancestors reinforces this ethical structure. Listening to the elders' advice, preserving the memory of those who came before, keeping the family's spiritual lineage alive are attitudes expressing humility and recognition. Wisdom is seen not as an exclusive product of reason or formal study, but as the fruit of lived experience and connection with the invisible world. Therefore, scorning elders or dishonoring one's origins was considered a sign of spiritual decay. Each generation is a guardian of a link in the sacred chain connecting past to future. Breaking this link is betraying Tengri's trust.

In social life, Tengriism values justice and the word as instruments of mediation. Tribal councils, composed of chiefs and shamans, resolved disputes based on dialogue and observation of spiritual signs. Truth was not just factual but carried a sacred dimension. Lying deliberately stained one's own soul, as it meant trying to deceive spirits and the Sky as well. This understanding gave great weight to words. Speaking required responsibility. Storytellers, bards, and shamans developed an eloquence imbued with ethics—they knew their words shaped reality, so they cared for them as if they were seeds.

In the relationship with animals and nature, Tengriist ethics reveal a sensitivity rare today. Every living being is endowed with spirit. Hunting, slaughtering, or harvesting are not trivial actions, but solemn moments requiring awareness and respect. The killed animal must be honored, its spirit appeased with prayers and gestures of gratitude. Wasting parts of the animal or causing unnecessary suffering is considered an insult to the species' guardian spirits. Medicinal plants are gathered after formal requests to the earth and with the certainty they will be used for beneficial purposes. Nothing is taken without giving something in return—be it an offering, a prayer, or the promise not to abuse.

Even natural phenomena—storms, droughts, eclipses—are understood as expressions of spiritual forces. Disrespecting nature is disrespecting the sacred. Therefore, many sustainability practices found support not in civil laws, but in spiritual beliefs: not felling sacred trees, not polluting rivers, not hunting during animals' gestation, respecting the land's regeneration times. This ecological ethic, rooted in spirituality, predates any modern concept of ecology by centuries and proves surprisingly relevant amidst contemporary environmental crises.

Ethics also permeate the practice of war, inevitable in nomadic life. The ideal warrior is not the bloodthirsty one, but the protector. Fighting for personal revenge or gratuitous plunder was condemnable. Combat was justified only when motivated by the defense of honor, family, or community. Even so, it was necessary to consult shamans, ask the sky for signs, and ensure the cause aligned with Tengri's will. Warriors relied on ancestral blessings, and after battles, paid tribute to the dead, whether friends or enemies. This spiritualization of war didn't eliminate violence but imposed moral limits and constantly reminded that spilled blood fell upon the soul of the spiller.

In modern times, this ancestral ethic finds renewed forms of expression. In urbanized and digitally connected societies, many adherents of Tengriism seek to rescue fundamental values by adapting them to modern life. Being honest in business, respecting cultural differences, cultivating strong family ties, consuming consciously, caring for the environment, helping others without expecting reward—all these are contemporary ways of living Tengri's ethic. More than rules, they are guidelines emerging from the inner feeling of connection with the whole.

It's important to highlight that, lacking a formal religious institution, Tengriism relies on individual conscience and spiritual self-regulation. Each person is responsible for seeking alignment with the Sky, guided by the heart, omens, and the teachings of the wiser ones. There are no eternal hells or feared final judgments—but there is the certainty that everything returns, everything balances. Doing good is, therefore, doing good to oneself. Living with honor, in harmony with others and nature, is the only way to remain at peace under the gaze of the Eternal Sky.

This reliance on conscience as a moral compass reveals a mature spirituality, where the individual is called to develop discernment and sensitivity towards life. It's not about following norms out of fear of punishment, but about cultivating deep listening—to the world, to ancestors, to the subtle signs of the spirit. Silence, dreams, repeating coincidences, a wise word from an elder: all can be guidance. Living ethically, in this horizon, means being attuned to a frequency that doesn't impose, but invites. Error, when it occurs, demands not public penance, but sincere recognition and genuine effort to restore harmony. Forgiveness isn't a concession; it's a necessity for the spirit not to carry unnecessary burdens on its journey.

It is this sense of free responsibility that makes Tengriism particularly relevant in a time when many question institutions and seek more authentic spiritualities. It proposes not an unattainable ideal, but a possible path, human, fallible, and sacred all at once. Values arise not to confine, but to guide—like trails opened by the example of those who came before. Honoring spirits requires not perfection, but coherence. It's not enough to proclaim love for nature while consuming unconsciously; it's insufficient to talk about ancestry without listening to the elders of one's own community. The modern Tengriist is called to unite intention and action, word and gesture, in every aspect of life.

Therefore, more than a moral code, Tengriism offers a pedagogy of being. It teaches that living with respect, courage, and generosity is more than a virtue—it's a way of keeping the world breathing. And if every action resonates in the invisible fabric connecting us, then every choice, however small, carries the potential for healing or wounding. The Eternal Sky doesn't judge with scales but observes constantly. And under that gaze, ethics cease to be an obligation and become an art—the art of living in tune with all that exists.

Chapter 29
Spiritual Identity

In the inner vastness extending beyond flesh and history, there is an invisible anchor binding the human being to something larger, something before birth and after death: this anchor is spiritual identity. For the peoples who lived under the infinite sky of the steppes, this identity was not an abstract concept or a distant philosophy—it pulsed in daily life, in war chants, in dawn prayers, in the whispers of mountains, and in the smell of milk boiling over the sacred fire. In Tengriism, rediscovering spiritual identity isn't just recalling the faith of ancestors; it's rediscovering who one is in totality, merging bloodline, land of origin, and cosmos into a single inner voice.

For centuries, this voice was muffled by empires, invasions, external doctrines, forced conversions, and assimilation policies. Shamanic traditions were marginalized, ancient names replaced by foreign designations, and rituals connecting with sky and earth silenced or ridiculed. However, even in the darkest periods, the spark of spiritual identity was not completely extinguished. It persisted in myths told by grandmothers, in automatic gestures of reverence to mountains, in instinctive respect for animals, and in silent tears shed before the starry sky. Tengriism survived as embodied memory—a collective spiritual body awaiting reanimation.

When repression eased and communities began revisiting their past, many realized something essential had been forgotten. It wasn't just about rituals or ancient gods, but about a way of being in the world, a way of seeing life and death, time and space. This spiritual awakening has manifested on various levels—from the political to the personal. Intellectuals began advocating for the valorization of cultural roots; artists started exploring Tengriist symbols in their works; families rediscovered stories that seemed dormant. But more profoundly, individuals began feeling an inner call to something they couldn't name, yet resonated with an ancestry deeper than genetics.

Assuming a Tengriist spiritual identity today is an act of courage and love. It's saying no to the homogenization imposed by institutionalized religions and globalizing cultural models. It's affirming that there is a collective soul that cannot be erased, and that this soul has a voice, a scent, a rhythm. In some cases, this manifests through adopting traditional names, reviving ceremonial garments, using ancient runes in tattoos or amulets. In others, it's a subtler internal shift: a way of praying silently to the sky, attentive listening to intuitions coming from the wind, reverence for the sunrise as a reunion with mystery.

This spiritual identity, however, isn't limited to ethnicity or territory. Although rooted in Turkic and Mongolic cultures, it transcends geographical borders.

Many descendants in the diaspora—living in Europe, America, or other parts of the world—have found in Tengriism a bridge to reconnect with a lost sense of belonging. Others, even without blood ties to nomadic peoples, feel drawn to this spirituality because they recognize in it a mirror of their own yearnings: freedom, reverence for nature, direct connection with the sacred, communion with ancestors. Tengriism, in this sense, offers a universal archetype of spiritual identity that welcomes both the children of the steppe and the modern orphans of tradition.

There's also a therapeutic aspect to reclaiming this identity. In an increasingly fragmented world, with individuals disoriented by existential crises, belonging to something larger than the ego becomes a vital need. Tengriist spiritual identity offers not just meaning, but direction. It says: "You are not alone. You are part of a lineage, a land, a sky. Your steps echo the steps of your ancestors. Your voice is a continuation of ancient songs. Your pain and joy have a place in the sacred circle of life." This message isn't dogma, but profound consolation.

The symbology of this identity is rich and alive. The blue color of the sky, the deep sound of the shamanic drum, the arc of light on the horizon at dawn, the distant bleating of herds, the name of a river holding memories of forgotten rites—all compose a spiritual grammar communicating with the heart. Reassuming this language is reconnecting with a deep memory, one perhaps never truly lost, only dormant. It's like hearing again a song that, unknowingly, has always been in our soul.

Importantly, this spiritual identity demands no exclusivity. Many who identify as Tengriists today continue to attend mosques, churches, or Buddhist temples. Tengriism requires no renunciation, only truth. It invites integration, reconciliation, recognition that behind many forms lies the same essence: the search for connection, meaning, and beauty. Thus, it doesn't conflict with other beliefs but illuminates them from an ancestral viewpoint. A Muslim understanding Tengri as the cosmic face of Allah, a Buddhist seeing Tengriist rituals as expressions of natural dharma, a Christian recognizing in the eternal sky the same creator God—all can drink from this spring without fear of heresy.

In times of identity crisis and excessive noise, Tengriist spiritual identity offers silence and presence. Silence to listen to the whispers of the invisible; presence to fully inhabit the body, the earth, time. It doesn't impose itself by force but reveals itself through beauty. It doesn't compete but invites. It doesn't close doors but opens paths—not outward, but inward. And in this inner dive, the individual rediscovers not only the gods of sky and earth but also their own true face.

This rediscovery, when collective, has even greater implications. Entire peoples, by resuming their native spirituality, regain self-esteem, dignity, and voice. Tengriism then becomes not just a religion, but a movement of historical healing. It restores to Turkic-Mongol peoples the possibility of telling their own narrative, no longer from the viewpoint of those who colonized or tried to convert them, but from their own myths, values, rhythm. And in doing so, they show the world it's possible to be modern without being amnesiac, global without being generic, spiritual without being alienated.

By restoring this spiritual identity, it's not just about returning to roots, but about a rebirth that updates the past without freezing it. Tengriism, by offering itself as a living path, allows each individual to reconnect with their essence without needing to deny the complexities of the present. It's a spirituality that breathes with time, accepts the plurality of the modern world, but doesn't relinquish ancestral depth. Spiritual identity, in this context, becomes a compass pointing inward, even when the world's winds blow in contrary directions. And by following this intimate direction, the human being finds solidity in a world of impermanence.

This solidity, however, doesn't manifest as rigidity, but as a center. A center from which one can walk freely, dialogue with others without fear of getting lost, love without fragmenting. Tengriist spirituality needn't assert itself by negating the different, because it's firmly rooted in what is essential. That's why it flourishes without pretensions of supremacy, and precisely why it touches so many hearts.

It's possible someone discovers their spiritual identity not amidst drums or chants, but in silent contemplation of a tree or the sudden recollection of a forgotten ancestral name. Recognition doesn't depend on form—it's an act of presence. Perhaps, ultimately, what Tengriism teaches about spiritual identity is the art of remembering who you are without needing to oppose anyone. To be whole, true, part—of the sky, the earth, history, and the future. This is the heritage the peoples of the steppes bequeathed to the world: the certainty that the soul has territory, voice, and purpose. And when this soul awakens, even in distant times and strange lands, it brings with it a breath of eternity that transforms everything around. The blue sky remains, silent and vast, as witness and guardian of each reunion.

Chapter 30
Sacred Connection

Beneath the serene mantle of the blue sky, where the wind dances among the hills and ancient echoes reverberate through the mountains, exists an invisible and eternal bond uniting all beings. This bond is not an imposed belief, nor a theological structure built by scholars. It is an experience pulsing at the core of Tengriist spirituality: the sacred connection. A way of being in the world that transcends the rational, depends neither on sacred texts nor religious hierarchies, but arises from the intimacy between the human spirit and the cosmos surrounding it. The sacred connection is the silent bridge linking the heart to the sky, the feet to the earth, and the soul to the divine breath permeating all things.

In Tengriism, this connection is innate. It's not something learned or earned, but something recognized. From a nomad's first steps on the steppe's damp grass, the world around whispers its sacredness. Each element—the fire that warms, the water that quenches, the mountain that watches, the sky that envelops—is perceived as part of a great living organism, a web of spiritual relationships sustaining universal balance. The human being, in this context, is not master of creation, but its child. And their deepest mission is to remember this every day, in every gesture, every thought.

This remembrance occurs through simple yet powerful rituals. Tossing milk to the sky at dawn isn't just cultural tradition—it's an act of gratitude and reverence. Tying blue ribbons to trees isn't folklore—it's acknowledging a spirit dwells there deserving respect. Sitting silently before a bonfire isn't just rest—it's living meditation, listening to the unseen. These gestures, small in appearance, are immense in meaning. They weave, thread by thread, the sacred connection between the individual and the universe. They rescue what was forgotten: that true spirituality isn't shouted, but whispered. Not imposed, but shared.

There's an inherent poetry in this form of spirituality. The sacred connection in Tengriism requires no temples—for the sky's dome is the greatest one. It demands no priests—for every being can dialogue directly with spirits. It's not limited to one day of the week or one season of the year—but manifests in the everyday, in breathing, walking, attentive gazing. It lies in how one treats an animal, harvests a plant, respects the silence of dawn. And above all, it lies in the awareness that every human action reverberates through the cosmic fabric—potentially strengthening or breaking the sacred ties binding us to all that lives.

For modern practitioners of Tengriism, this sacred connection has taken on new contours. Amidst urban concrete and technological noise, there's a conscious effort to reclaim this spiritual relationship with the world. Many find in urban nature—a solitary tree, sudden rain, a bird's flight—points of contact with the invisible. Others seek parks, forests, or mountains on weekends not just for leisure, but as silent pilgrimage. And there are those who, even in cramped apartments, light candles, maintain altars with stones, herbs, ancestor photos, creating microcosms of sacredness where only emptiness existed. In these gestures, the ancestral spirit of Tengriism manifests in new forms—adapted, yet alive.

The sacred connection also has a profound psychological aspect. In times of anxiety, loneliness, and fragmentation, it offers an effective antidote. By reconnecting with the natural and spiritual world, the individual rediscovers their own wholeness. They feel part of something larger, guided by forces unseen but felt. Many report mystical experiences under the starry sky—a feeling of fullness, cosmic belonging, inner peace that no rational explanation can contain. This expanded state of consciousness, common in shamanic practices, isn't delusion, but reunion with the sacred dimension of existence. It is the return to the center.

In Tengriism, there is no separation between the sacred and the profane. Everything is sacred—if lived consciously. Eating, sleeping, working, sexuality, raising children, aging—all life cycles are parts of a grand cosmic ceremony. And the sacred connection expresses itself precisely in this integration: one need not flee the world to find the divine. It is here, now, in the smell of wet earth, the sound of wind through leaves, the touch of a friendly hand. Recognizing this is awakening. Living this is honoring the legacy of ancestors.

The transmission of this spirituality occurs not through indoctrination, but by example. A child who sees their parents tossing milk to the sky, grows up hearing stories of mountain spirits, learns to ask permission from a tree before cutting a branch—this child internalizes the world's sacredness. And even if urban life momentarily distances them from it, the seed of sacred connection will be planted in their soul, ready to bloom when the time comes. Tengriism thus perpetuates itself not through institutional structures, but through lived gestures, bodily memory, ritual affection.

Importantly, this connection isn't just with the visible. It extends to ancestors, spirits of the dead, invisible protectors inhabiting subtle planes. For Tengriists, ancestors haven't died—they just moved residence. They accompany the living, guide, protect, teach. And keeping this link alive—through prayers, offerings, remembrances—is also keeping one's own identity alive. The sacred connection, therefore, is also a bridge between times. It unites past to present and prepares the ground for the future.

There's a silent yet powerful teaching in how ancient Mongols or Turks regarded the sky. They called it Tengri—but represented it with no image. The sky was God's own face, bare, infinite, blue. Looking at it was prayer. And this reminds us that sacred connection needs no intermediaries. It lies in the attentive gaze, the open heart, full presence. It lies in the silence that listens and the word that blesses. It lies, above all, in the humility of recognizing we are dust and star simultaneously—small before the universe, yet indispensable to its harmony.

Today, walking among ruins of extinct cultures or abandoned temples, one can feel that true spirituality doesn't die. It just changes clothes, language, dwelling. Tengriism, by offering the direct experience of sacred connection, shows that rebuilding grand structures isn't necessary to live the sacred. One simply needs to relearn how to listen. Remember. Reconnect with the earth, the sky, the ancestral flame still burning silently within each human being.

This act of reconnection, when lived sincerely, restores to daily life a brilliance that modern haste tends to extinguish. Every moment can become rite, every place an altar. Sacredness lies not in objects themselves, but in the gaze consecrating them. The child playing in mud, the elder contemplating sunset, the woman singing while preparing food—all participate in an invisible liturgy, where the entire world becomes a living temple. Tengriism reminds us there's no distance between spirit and life; that authentic spirituality isn't exception, but permanence. And that the divine reveals itself, above all, in the wholeness of small gestures.

With this understanding, existence transforms. Sacred connection demands neither isolation nor asceticism, but radical presence. It isn't achieved by fleeing human responsibilities, but by integrating them into sacred consciousness. Being a child of sky and earth implies living with loving responsibility: caring, protecting, thanking. The bond with the invisible doesn't distance from matter—on the contrary, it makes matter a channel for spiritual expression. And thus, touching the earth can be blessing. Caring for someone can be prayer. Working with dedication can be offering. Life ceases to be burden and becomes gift—when lived with a soul awake to the mystery permeating everything.

The sacred connection, ultimately, is less a path to be tread and more a state to be remembered. It's a return to what was always present, even when forgotten. In inner silence, in memories surfacing without reason, in the sudden urge to contemplate the sky—therein lies the call. And answering this call requires no credentials or masters, only surrender. Tengriism, with its ancestral wisdom, invites us to live sacredly without separating the spiritual from the human. To weave, with the thread of consciousness, a bridge between what we are and what we always were. Under the Eternal Sky, all is united—and remembering this is, perhaps, the highest of rituals.

Chapter 31
Modern Re-signification

As the sands of time slip silently across the vast steppes of history, Tengriism—that ancient and vital spirituality of the Turkic and Mongol peoples—does not disappear. It transforms. It doesn't fade under modern winds but resurfaces in new forms, like embers persisting beneath the ashes of forgetfulness. And in this silent resurrection, the process of re-signification takes crucial shape. Ancestral wisdom isn't left behind; it is transcribed, adapted, reinterpreted, as if ancient songs gained new instruments. The 21st century, with its dizzying speed and unprecedented existential challenges, demands this movement of recreating the sacred, and Tengriism responds with surprising vitality.

Re-signifying, in this context, isn't distorting. It's translating. It's taking yesterday's symbols and giving them new contours without stripping their essence. An *ovoo* built on a mountain remains a point of connection with spirits—but can now ally with an ecological cause, as a symbol of nature protection. A shamanic drum, once a tool for trance, also becomes a therapeutic instrument in contemporary emotional healing sessions. Celestial gods and earth spirits need not be seen as literal beings for their message to touch deeply. They can be archetypes, forces of the psyche, living metaphors. The mountain spirit can be both an invisible entity and the symbolic expression of the landscape's own majesty, stability, ancestry. This plasticity of Tengriism is its greatest strength. Unlike dogmatic systems demanding orthodoxy, it allows fluidity.

A young Kazakh with a scientific mind can look at Tengri and see the cosmos, the quantum field, universal order. An urban Mongolian woman can see in Umay not a goddess, but the representation of her maternal intuition, the force protecting her children in the city's chaos. Thus, the ancient faith doesn't fossilize—it pulses between the lines of modern life, like a subterranean river erupting where least expected.

Language also participates in this symbolic rebirth. Ancestral terms are rescued, but with new nuances. Words like *kut*, *sülde*, *tör* gain space in conversations, blogs, music, even political discourse, not as ethnographic relics, but as living words naming intimate experiences. Some call their vital energy *kut* instead of "soul" or "spirit." Some refer to their personal dignity as *tör*, evoking ancient clan moral codes. This symbolic vocabulary restores spiritual density to daily existence. Speaking these terms is also invoking a collective memory that still vibrates, even beneath layers of globalized modernity.

The educational field, in turn, offers a promising arena for re-signifying Tengriism. Schools in Mongolia, Kazakhstan, and Buryatia have included elements of native mythology and spirituality in their curricula. Teachers explain the meaning of rituals, tell ancestral legends, and promote visits to sacred sites. But they do so to integrate, not exclude. Tengri isn't presented as an exclusive alternative to established religions, but as part of the peoples' spiritual and identity heritage. With this, generations raised alienated from their roots begin to see in them not backwardness, but strength. And they feel pride in the blue sky their ancestors worshipped—not as nostalgia, but as recognition.

In the arts, the process is even more intense. Musicians blend electronic beats with shamanic throat singing, creating a sound vibrating between past and future. Filmmakers revisit heroic narratives where protagonists hear omens in the winds and make offerings to fire before battle. Painters depict celestial gods with modern strokes, reinterpreting their features according to present dilemmas. And writers, especially poets, have rescued traditional spiritual vocabulary as a source of existential inspiration. In their words, the sky isn't just scenery—it's character, witness, silent judge.

In cities, youth groups gather to perform Tengriist ceremonies—but with innovations. Sometimes no traditional shaman is present, but a facilitator who studied ancestral practices and adapts them respectfully. The drum is played alongside computers. Blue ribbons are tied not to sacred trees, but to concrete balconies. And yet, the spirit manifests. Because the essential remains: the sincere intention of reconnection, silent gratitude to the sky, reverence for the earth. This reveals Tengriism's power—its ability to mold to context without losing its vibrant core.

One cannot ignore that this modern re-signification raises debates. Some critics accuse urban practitioners of "diluting" the tradition, turning the sacred into spectacle or boutique therapy. Others, more conservative, reject any adaptation and clamor for a "pure" return to archaic rituals. But time shows it is precisely adaptation that ensures survival. The Tengriism flourishing today isn't a copy of the past, but its dynamic continuity. It incorporates, transforms, integrates. It doesn't close itself in dogmas but opens to interpretations. And in this movement, it educates—not by imposition, but by enchantment.

Science, far from being an enemy, also finds points of contact with this renewed spirituality. Studies on holistic health, transpersonal psychology, and the neuroscience of meditation recognize the benefits of practices inspired by shamanism. The rhythmic beat of the drum, for example, has proven effects on brain synchronization. Gratitude rituals reduce stress. Contact with nature improves mental health. Thus, what the ancients knew through experience, science confirms through experimentation. And this doesn't empty the mystery—it just expands awareness.

Technology, initially seeming opposed to the ancestral spirit, can also serve as a vehicle. Social networks have become spaces for disseminating Tengriist teachings. Videos explain myths, podcasts interview shamans, apps mark solstice celebration dates. There are even video games with plots based on Turco-Mongol cosmology. This attracts youth, who feel part of something ancient and new simultaneously. It's an unlikely but possible marriage: ancestry and innovation. The eternal sky finds its reflection on digital screens—not as substitute, but as echo.

Tengriist ethics also find expression in modern causes. Environmental groups inspired by respect for nature spirits fight against forest and river destruction. Indigenous and cultural movements promote the valorization of ancestral knowledge, partly fueled by spiritual rebirth. And there are even attempts to integrate Tengriism into proposals for ethical governance—with leaders evoking values like the honored word, hospitality, community sense. The old ideal of ruling in the Sky's name, as legitimate khagans did, resurfaces in discourses on ecological responsibility and social justice.

Modern Tengriism, therefore, is not a religion in the Western sense. It is a spirituality in constant re-signification. A symbolic fabric expanding according to the needs of the contemporary soul. It demands no blind faith but invites experience. It imposes no dogmas but inspires questions. And perhaps that's why it's resurging with such force—because today's world, saturated with certainties, yearns for meaning. And this meaning, as the ancients knew, can be found in the wind blowing from the east, the fire dancing in silence, the sky that never stopped watching over us.

This force of re-signification manifests, above all, in how Tengriism touches individual lives, awakening memories not just personal, but collective, deep, often inexplicable. It's not a simple revival of customs, but an inner movement seeking to restore the link between the human being and mystery. Each adaptation made reverently doesn't diminish the tradition—it renews it, allowing the essence to remain alive wherever it may be. The sacred meaning, so dear to the Tengriist spirit, resides not in fixed forms, but in the ability to listen to the invisible and respond authentically. And that's why, even in the most urbanized environments, this spirituality continues to flourish with strength and coherence.

At the same time, this modern spiritual rebirth doesn't erase challenges. There are natural tensions between tradition and innovation, between the yearning for purity and the need for evolution. But what Tengriism demonstrates is that fidelity to origin lies not in preserving every detail, but in keeping alive the breath animating the whole. This breath leads youth to beat drums in apartments, inspires teachers to tell forgotten legends, guides activists to fight for rivers and forests as if fighting for their own souls.

Re-signifying, therefore, is an act of spiritual courage—believing the sacred can be reborn, even when seemingly buried under noise and concrete. In the vastness of a transforming world, Tengriism resurfaces not as relic, but as response. It seeks neither to win religious disputes nor occupy institutional power spaces. It offers a way of listening, an ethic of belonging, a spirituality shaping itself to time without bowing to it. And as long as there are those who look to the sky and feel a call, touch the earth reverently, hear a drum and feel their heart align with the cosmos' rhythm—

Tengriism will continue, re-signified yet whole, like an ancient breath recognizing itself in the future.

Chapter 32
Ancestral Wisdom

Far beyond any written doctrine, the essence of Tengriism resides in a living wisdom, passed down through generations like an ancestral melody, silently transmitted between drumbeats, chants murmured to the wind, and decisions made in the shade of a sacred tree. This wisdom claims no systematization, nor imposes itself through dogmas—it exists as a field of presence, fertile ground where every daily gesture carries a teaching, and where Earth, Sky, spirits, and ancestors speak through symbols, signs, and rhythms. This form of knowing, sometimes ignored or underestimated, is precisely what best escapes the erosion of time: subtle yet resilient wisdom that survived the invasion of empires, forced religious conversions, and corrosive modernity.

The ancestral wisdom of Tengriism begins not with a prophet or a book. It begins with the attentive gaze of the hunter understanding the wind's movement and the prey's silence; with the herder's ear distinguishing signs of contentment or alarm in the cattle's voice; with the mother observing the sky before giving birth, trusting the child arrives under good omens. It begins with the old man's gesture pouring milk onto the ground at dawn, honoring Mother Earth, and with the child learning fire isn't just heat, but spirit. These practices shape a knowledge not taught in schools, but etched into the body, senses, heart. Knowledge more breathed than learned.

Within this invisible framework of teachings, the ancients distinguished various types of soul—each with its role and destiny. Knowing which soul fell ill or departed was as important as diagnosing a fever. It was this plural view of being that taught one cannot treat the body without touching the spirit, nor care for the mind without reconciling with ancestors. Wisdom, in Tengriism, is aligning the multiple layers of being: the *nefes* (breath), the *sülde* (identity soul), the *kut* (vital force), and the spirit wandering in dreams. Each ancestral term carries centuries of observation of human nature, condensed into myths and metaphors. And it is through these myths—never closed, always open to symbol—that the steppe peoples understood their relationship with the cosmos.

The Tengriist worldview proposes the universe is in constant dialogue with itself. The three worlds—upper, middle, lower—are not watertight compartments, but permeable dimensions, linked by roots and branches of a World Tree that also grows within the human being. This symbolic tree, whose roots touch the spirits of the underworld and whose crown reaches the celestial spheres, is an inner map. On it, one learns balance isn't achieved by denying the depths nor reached solely by aiming for heights. True wisdom lies in knowing how to ascend and descend, like the shaman traveling between worlds to bring healing. The image of the shaman dancing around the fire is, in this sense, an archetype of integration: he doesn't flee the world but dives into it, to reintegrate the fragmented, retrieve what was lost, restore harmony.

This wisdom also reveals itself in language. Ancient proverbs—transmitted as songs, refrains, or warnings—encapsulate lessons of survival, respect, and compassion. The elders said: "Don't cut the tree that gives you shade," or "The horse doesn't laugh at the fallen mountain, for tomorrow it may rise again." These seemingly simple phrases carry echoes of a profound ethic, rooted in reciprocity. The forest protects those who respect it. The river gives back to those who don't pollute it. The animal surrendering to the hunter is remembered, not forgotten. Living well, in this symbolic universe, means living in relation—with visible and invisible beings, with the living and those departed. Therefore, offering rituals are not mere formalities, but gestures of gratitude and cosmic balance.

There is also therapeutic wisdom inscribed in shamanic practices. The notion that spiritual traumas manifest as physical or psychic illnesses is millennia-old in Tengriism, long before modern psychology formulated the concept of "somatization." The shaman, by sucking an "intrusive object" from a sick person's body or returning their lost soul after a fright, performs a type of symbolic healing that still resonates today with practices of transpersonal psychology or energy medicine. There are records of sessions where modern patients, even without understanding Tengriist cosmology, experience profound relief participating in these rituals. This is because symbolic language accesses areas of consciousness reason cannot reach. The soul, as the ancients knew, responds better to songs than arguments.

The ancestral wisdom of Tengriism also manifests in the relationship with time. Time, for the spiritual nomad, is not linear. It is cyclical, spiraled, seasonal. Each season brings a teaching: spring renews, summer celebrates, autumn prepares, and winter gathers. Living according to this time means learning to listen to nature's rhythms and inner rhythms. There's a time to plant and a time not to plant; a time to speak and a time to be silent; a time to act and a time to listen. This rhythmic knowledge is vital in an era where everything is urgent. Tengriism teaches the pause, the rite, the sacred interval. And thus, by rescuing its wisdom, we also rescue another way of inhabiting time—more connected, more respectful, more whole.

Myths, in this process, are not mere ancient stories. They are symbolic pedagogies. The myth of Erlik, descending to lower worlds and trying to steal Ulgen's creation, is a narrative of ambivalence and learning: evil isn't just punishment, but also teacher. The story of the blue she-wolf guiding Turkic ancestors from destruction to rebirth is an account of resilience, motherhood, and inner direction. These myths, told around the fire for generations, aren't fantasy—they are maps of the soul. And when someone modern hears, reads, or experiences these stories in a ritual or performance, something reactivates. It's as if the species' deep memory—the one connecting us to Earth—awakens.

Today, universities and research centers begin recognizing this ancestral wisdom not as folklore, but as a complex knowledge system. Anthropologists, psychologists, philosophers rediscover in Tengriism keys to understanding pre-modern spirituality and, paradoxically, paths for the future. Because there's an increasingly clear truth: technical progress isn't enough. We need spiritual horizons. And ancestral traditions like Tengriism offer not just religious content—they offer ontologies, ways of being, perspectives on life challenging the dominant paradigm.

Returning to this wisdom, however, requires more than study. It requires listening. It requires the modern world to silence for a moment its noises of efficiency and results, and allow itself to hear the whisper of fire, the swaying of trees, the flight of the falcon. This listening is the door to what the ancients called the "voice of the Sky." And though one cannot prove this voice, whoever hears it knows it exists. It's the voice saying: you belong. You are connected. You have a place in life's circle.

This listening, when cultivated humbly, becomes a portal to another form of knowledge—more intuitive, more experiential, less anxious for control. The ancestral wisdom of Tengriism doesn't ask one to understand everything, but to be present. To walk respectfully, speak intentionally, listen with the whole body. In times of fragmentation and empty hyperconnection, this wisdom reappears as silent medicine, a reminder of wholeness. Those allowing themselves to be touched by it rediscover that learning isn't accumulating, but awakening. And that there's a knowing revealed only in relation: with elements, others, the invisible.

In this movement, rescuing ancestral wisdom means returning not to the past as museum, but as source. It's diving into roots to bloom authentically in the present. Youth approaching Tengriism often do so seeking identity, but end up discovering also a sense of direction and belonging transcending the individual. And it's at this point that the ancients' wisdom proves itself alive: it dictates no ready paths, but guides one to look at the sky, feel the ground, recognize signs, and decide with a heart aligned to the cosmos. This cannot be taught in formulas—but it can be lived. And, when lived, transforms.

The ancestral wisdom of Tengriism reminds us being wise isn't accumulating answers, but cultivating presence. That honoring ancestors is also transforming the world so they would recognize it as worthy. That hearing the "voice of the Sky" isn't a privilege of few, but the right and responsibility of all breathing beneath it. In a world increasingly eager for quick solutions, this ancestral tradition offers something deeper: a way of being that doesn't separate knowing from feeling, nor human from sacred. And perhaps this is what we need most now—not more knowledge, but wisdom. And that, as the ancients knew, is born from silence, listening, and walking with Sky and Earth in the heart. For as the steppe elders said, "the sky's knowing isn't written—it's breathed." And breathing it, today, is a way to resist, remember, and be reborn. Under the same blue sky.

Chapter 33
Cosmic Harmony

The journey through the spiritual universe of Tengriism leads us, without maps or promises, to the perception that everything existing pulses with the same primordial rhythm. There is no word more precise for this rhythm than harmony. Not an illusory harmony, made of immutable order and imposed silence, but a living, vibrant harmony, changeable like the wind on the steppes, recognizing conflict and transition as parts of existence's dynamic balance. In Tengriism, this cosmic harmony isn't just a philosophical ideal—it's an experienceable reality, lived through the connection between the human being, the natural world, and the invisible forces traversing both.

The essence of Tengriism has always been relational. The human being doesn't exist as a separate entity; they are child of Earth and Sky, sibling of animals, cousin of trees, nephew of mountains. This implies a cosmic responsibility: to live is to actively participate in a network of relationships extending beyond what eyes can reach. In this context, every action has spiritual consequence. Pouring milk at dawn isn't an empty symbolic gesture, but recognition of the flow of gifts between what's received and what's returned. Offering tobacco to the soil, lighting fire reverently, calling a guardian spirit by name—all are ways to keep the dance of balance alive.

Cosmic harmony also expresses itself in the tripartite cosmology underpinning shamanic thought: the middle world, where we live; the upper world, home to luminous forces and order; and the lower world, where mysteries, shadows, and forces healing through confrontation reside. Between these worlds, there's no rigid separation, but constant interpenetration. It's in this back-and-forth that the shaman's wisdom resides: ascending to heavens for messages, descending to the underworld to rescue souls, returning to the material plane to restore health and order. Cosmic harmony manifests in the fluidity with which planes touch, without absolute hierarchy, without exclusion. Each world has its role, and scorning any is breaking the balance.

It's from this perspective that the importance of ritual is understood. Ritual is the thread weaving worlds. In it, ordinary time suspends, opening a sacred time-space where cosmic harmony can be restored or reinforced. When a drum resonates under the starry night and a voice intones ancestors' names, it's not nostalgia, but reconnection. What was scattered begins to converge: living and dead, human and non-human, visible and invisible. Ritual rebalances not only external elements, but also internal ones—parts of the being in dissonance start hearing each other again.

In daily life, this harmony translates into simple actions, yet laden with intention. The shepherd thanking the flock before slaughter, the farmer planting by moon phases, the elder woman whispering blessings into tea offered to grandchildren. These gestures sustain a world not cut into pieces, but remaining whole. And this whole world isn't less real for being invisible to distracted eyes. On the contrary: it sustains everything else.

Cosmic harmony also demands listening. Listening to what speaks without words: the silence of mountains, the murmur of rivers, the whisper of fire. In Tengriism, learning to listen is perhaps the most fundamental virtue. Listening to nature's signs, dreams, omens. Listening to one's own intuition as if it were an allied spirit's speech. Listening to elders not just with ears, but with body, time, humility. Because it's in listening that the soul learns its place within the vastness.

In practical terms, this listening translates into specific ways of acting in the world. Respectful agriculture not exhausting the soil. Ceremonial hunting recognizing the animal's gift. Architecture oriented by sun and winds. Music tuned to nature's sounds. All these aspects, though seeming technical or functional, are expressions of a greater harmony—the one existing between human making and the universe's intelligence.

Tengriism also teaches this harmony isn't something achieved once and for all. It's fragile, transient, requiring constant maintenance. Like a horse needing daily brushing, like fire needing fuel, harmony needs attention, renewal, care. This means the human being is co-author of cosmic order. Not mere spectator, nor dominator, but active participant. A gardener of the invisible. And this implies responsibility, vigilance, and above all, devotion.

In the modern world, where everything is fragmented, accelerated, quantified, this notion of cosmic harmony might seem romantic or naive. But one only needs to look at crises—environmental, spiritual, social—to perceive the current imbalance isn't technical, it's ontological. A vision of totality, an ethic of care, a spirituality recognizing the other—be it human, animal, or mountain—as sacred is missing. Tengriism offers this vision. Not as a closed system, but as a horizon from which other forms of life are possible.

And perhaps most importantly: this harmony isn't a distant utopia. It can be touched now, this very instant, by breathing consciously, looking at the sky reverently, touching the earth respectfully. Every human being carries within them the possibility of becoming a bridge between worlds, an axis of balance. The shaman, in this sense, isn't just an external figure, but an internal function. Everyone can be their own shaman, provided they accept the call of Sky and Earth, and are willing to walk between shadows and lights with courage and humility.

In the end, what Tengriism teaches isn't a set of beliefs, but a way of being in the world. A way seeing in the sky a living presence, in the earth a nurturing mother, in winds messengers, in animals companions, in rivers masters. A way celebrating cycles, honoring the dead, singing to spirits, dancing with stars. A way reminding that life isn't separate from spirituality—it itself is the rite, the temple, the offering.

Living in cosmic harmony, within the Tengriist view, means recognizing oneself as part of an invisible symphony where each being has its note, its measure, its unique melody. When this recognition occurs, even the simplest gesture—like walking barefoot on grass or looking up at the sky before sleep—becomes prayer. This form of spirituality seeks not to transcend the world, but to inhabit it wholly. Harmony, thus, isn't distant abstraction, but embodied practice: it's in how one breathes, speaks, harvests, silences. And this practice renews daily, because balance is movement, never fixed state.

This awareness of belonging denies neither pain nor chaos, but welcomes them as part of the flow. Thunder has as much place as breeze. Loss also teaches, emptiness also speaks. Understanding this, the practitioner of Tengriism learns to walk lightly among forces they cannot control, but with which they can dialogue. Life then ceases to be battle against destiny and becomes dance with mystery. It's this understanding giving depth to cosmic harmony: it demands not perfection, only presence. Not certainties, only surrender. It sustains itself not on force, but on listening, care, constant return to center.

By recognizing everything is relation—with sky, earth, spirits, other beings, oneself—the individual reclaims their sacred place in life's circle. And in this circle, no one is more important than another, no one is above or below: all participate in the same breath, the same cosmic dance. This is the lesson echoing softly in Tengriism's practices, myths, songs, silences. A lesson which, though ancestral, remains alive because it pulses wherever someone stops to listen to the wind and remember life isn't separate from the sacred—it *is* the sacred, in its fullest form.

Epilogue

It is not possible to emerge unscathed from a crossing like the one you have just made. What this book has revealed are not just ancient practices or forgotten fragments of an ancestral culture — they are keys to a spirituality that still pulsates, silently, through the veils of the modern world. And now that these keys have been handed to you, something within you has changed. Perhaps discreetly, like the wind changing direction. Perhaps intensely, like the fire that consumes and purifies.

Tengrism, as presented here, does not demand a literal return to the steppes, the tents, or the shamanic rituals of yesteryear. The true return it proposes is internal. It is a re-encounter with the essence that has always been present, but which has been muffled by the noise of haste, disconnection, and collective forgetfulness. Because, at its deepest root, this wisdom does not belong only to the Turco-Mongolic peoples: it belongs to the human being. To the being who recognizes the sky with reverence, who touches the earth with care, who listens to the ancestors with humility, and who walks with awareness between worlds.

The teachings gathered here do not end with the last page. On the contrary, it is from this point that they begin to bear fruit. Throughout this reading, you were guided through spiritual landscapes where the sky was not a metaphor, but presence; where the earth was not a resource, but mother; where the spirits were not legends, but subtle companions. Each concept presented is a seed. And like every seed, it needs time, listening, shade, and light. And above all, continuity.

The spirituality proposed here does not separate, does not hierarchize, does not divide. It unites. It unites the visible and the invisible, the body and the soul, the human and the non-human. In this cosmovision, the sacred is not an exception to routine — it is the very fabric of life. And understanding this is understanding that every gesture matters. That every word spoken under the sky is heard. That every decision, even the most intimate, reverberates between the worlds.

Throughout these pages, you have walked alongside shamans, kings, and elders. You have listened to the wind that carries the forgotten songs. You have learned that there is no sin, but imbalance; that there is no promised salvation, but harmony achieved day by day. You have learned that honoring the ancestors is more than lighting incense: it is living in such a way as not to shame them. That caring for the earth is more than an ecological act: it is a form of spiritual gratitude.

But perhaps the greatest teaching is this: the sky never moved away from us — it was we who stopped looking at it. The good news is that the sky is still there. And it is still willing to listen. The return to true spirituality, therefore, does not require great reforms or escapes from civilization. It demands, rather, an intimate reconnection with silence, with the body, with the natural flow of life. It demands attention. Reverence. Listening.

The memory of the nomadic soul is, ultimately, an invitation to lightness. To live with less noise, less rigidity, less arrogance. And with more listening, more presence, more attunement to the cycles. The nomad knew they were not the center of the world — they were part of it. They knew that the invisible forces did not demand fear, but respect. They knew that destiny is written with feet on the ground and eyes on the heavens.

And now you know too.

Tengrism does not propose that you abandon everything, but that you review your way of being in the world. It teaches that spirituality is, above all, quality of presence. It is in the way you sit before a bonfire or before a stranger. It is in the way you breathe, how you listen, how you act when no one is watching. It is in the decision to live as part of the whole — and not as its owner.

As you close this book, something remains open. A cycle has ended, but the spiritual path does not close. It merely becomes more visible, more accessible. You can now recognize the signs with more clarity. You can listen more deeply. You can, ultimately, live with more meaning. Because the knowledge accessed here is not meant to be merely read. It asks to be lived.

And that begins now. In the simplest gesture, in the most honest word, in the most attentive gaze towards the sky. What the ancients knew — and what this book has reminded you — is that true spirituality does not need to be taught, only awakened. And if it has awakened in you, even if only in flashes, then it has already been worthwhile.

Remember: you are part of the lineage that contemplates the sky and recognizes the earth as sacred. You are part of the current that did not break, only fell asleep. And now awakens. The journey continues, and the drum still sounds. May your listening be deep, may your steps be light, and may your soul, like the ancients, know how to dance between the worlds with wisdom.

May the Eternal Sky inspire you. May Mother Earth sustain you. May the ancestral spirits accompany you. Always.

www.ingramcontent.com/pod-product-compliance
Lightning Source LLC
LaVergne TN
LVHW041931070526
838199LV00051BA/2769